TRADITIONAL HOME™

TRADITIONAL HOME™
Editor: Karol DeWulf Nickell
Art Director: Marisa Dirks
Managing Editor: John Riha
Home and Garden Editor: Mike Butler
Products and Design Editor: Carla Breer Howard
Features Editor: Dan Weeks
Interior Design Editor: Pamela J. Wilson
Copy Chief/Production Editor: Michael Diver
Associate Art Director: Terri Ketcham
Senior Grapic Designer: Kelly Barton
Contributing Editor, Food: Janet Figg
Contributing Editor, Antiques: Heather J. Wright
Editorial Assistant: Tina Meadows
Art Assistant: Sandee Roberts

Publisher: Deborah Jones Barrow

MEREDITH DESIGN GROUP
Vice President/Editorial Director: Dorothy Kalins
Vice President/Publishing Director: Stephen R. Burzon
Editorial Services Director: Charla Lawhon

President/Magazine Group: William T. Kerr

BETTER HOMES AND GARDENS® **BOOKS**
President, Book Group: Joseph J. Ward
Vice President and Editorial Director: Elizabeth P. Rice
Vice President, Retail Marketing: Jamie L. Martin
Vice President, Book Clubs: Richard L. Rundall

TRADITIONAL HOME™
Editor: Karol DeWulf Nickell
Project Editor: Marsha Jahns
Graphic Designer: Harijs Priekulis
Electronic Text Processor: Paula Forest

First Edition. Printing Number and Year: 5 4 3 2 1   96 95 94 93 92
ISSN: 1052-4398   ISBN: 0-696-01964-7

$\mathcal{W}$elcome to the 1992 collection of beautifully decorated homes from the pages of TRADITIONAL HOME™ magazine. This has been a bountiful year for interior

design. Classic traditional decorating styles are more popular than ever and more personal than ever. In this book, you'll meet people who, like you, take great pride in making their homes comfortable, elegant, and unique. While they've all chosen traditional style to be their design choice, each has interpreted it in a very special way. Our stories tell their stories and give you lots of decorating ideas for your own home in the bargain. Enjoy!

Karol DeWulf Nickell

February

City life agrees with Minneapolis designer Brian Ellingson. When he outgrew his first condominium, he bought two adjoining units 11 floors above, knocked down a few walls, and fashioned a modern penthouse in classic style.

Moving Up

BY HEATHER WRIGHT

PHOTOGRAPHY BY SUSAN GILMORE
PRODUCED BY SHARON ROSS

It was 10 years ago that designer Brian Ellingson bought his first Minneapolis condominium. It was a small, lackluster affair with low ceilings and an uninspired floor plan. With distinctive furnishings and a sense of adventure, though, Brian turned it into an elegant and very personal space. After eight years there, however, Brian's social life and passion for collecting antiques had long outgrown the modest abode; he began to feel anxious. "I longed for open, free-flowing space for entertaining," Brian says. "I wanted a gallery for my art. I wanted grandeur."

When two adjoining units 11 floors above him came up for sale at the same time, Brian knew it was his big break. He bought both

After remodeling two adjoining apartments into one, Brian, above, *added architectural detail to create a rich backdrop for his furniture and collections. The living room's new moldings and columns,* left, *are painted a glossy ecru that complements the mellow khaki walls and lend a subtly rich aesthetic.*

*I ARRANGE FURNITURE TO FACILITATE
CONVERSATION. IN THE LIVING ROOM THERE ARE
TWO INTIMATE AREAS: ONE AROUND THE SOFA,
ANOTHER NEXT TO THE FIREPLACE.*

— BRIAN ELLINGSON

MOVING UP

apartments, tore down some walls, and set about fashioning the modern penthouse in classic high style. In the process, he got free-flowing space and an art gallery. As for grandeur, he certainly made adequate allowances for that, too.

Brian's new apartment is now idyllic, but it took months to accomplish. "I had to gut much of it and start over again in order to make it work for me," he says. "And I soon found out that when you remodel a high-rise condo, you face challenges you don't in a typical house." Eight-inch-thick concrete walls and drywall riveted to metal studs rather than nailed to wood were just two of those challenges. "To top it all off," he adds, "everything

Brian designed a spacious dining room, left, *for his new apartment. "I love to create drop-dead table settings," he says. "I dim the chandelier, use lots of votive candles, glittering china, crystal, and silver, and top it off with exotic flowers." The lush trompe l'oeil by artist Carolynee Darling,* above, *is a reminder of Brian's love of the tropics and also expands the living room.*

MOVING UP

had to go into garbage cans and be taken down eighteen floors to be dumped!"

Because he wanted the apartment to remain comfortable as he matured, Brian made a significant investment in expensive details. "I really concentrated on the apartment's architectural nature in order to create a rich backdrop for my furniture and collections," he explains. To see his living room is to understand his rationale. By tearing down interior walls and using columns and soffits to define various areas, Brian gave an originally characterless space intrinsic charm and richness. He heightened the effect by trimming the living room and dining room with

The color scheme for the great-room, shown here, was derived from the Chinese rug used on the floor. The crisp blue in it is reinforced by Brian's collection of blue-and-white porcelain and by a needlepoint rug that hangs behind part of the neutral sectional sofa. Brian hunted for two years before he found the washed pine buffet at right. He now uses it as his media center.

MOVING UP

I FEEL A KINSHIP WITH HOW
THE ENGLISH GENTRY LIVED. THEIR
COUNTRY HOMES HAD AN
AURA OF ELEGANCE.

———— BRIAN ELLINGSON

crown molding and masking the dining room's small windows
behind floor-to-ceiling plantation shutters.

Brian carried the same attention to detail to other rooms, such
as the study. There, an antique mantel establishes an old-world
mood and inspired the styling of the wood paneling, bookshelves,
and molding for the rest of the room. Using antique and family
pieces, he's given the space its own distinctive character. An
antique music stand inherited from his aunt is used as a combina-
tion bookrack and bar. A collection of porcelain dogs by Royal
Doulton romps atop the mantel and bookshelves; more canine
affinity is reflected by antique oil paintings of dogs.

While enamored with the grace of the past, Brian isn't held
hostage by it. He wedded a vintage French-style chair from a
secondhand store with a bold tropical print for unexpected punch

The library right *evolved around an antique mahogany mantel
found in a consignment shop. Brian hung plantation shutters,
added mahogany paneling and bookshelves, and decorated in
rich greens. The window seat* above *converts to a bed. "This
room is like a womb," Brian says. "When I'm feeling beaten up
by the world, I come here to hide out and unwind."*

MOVING UP

in the living room. Because the scale and color of the print make it so strong, Brian limited its use to the chair and a couple of pillows. "Had I used more, the print would no longer be special," he says.

Though his apartment is utterly elegant, Brian is already looking forward to new projects. "This is just the start," he says. "I am constantly refining and upgrading, but only as my budget allows."

Though Brian is humble regarding his design accomplishments, he unwittingly gives himself the best possible compliment when he says, sitting in his apartment now, "There are many times I forget I'm living in an apartment eighteen floors above the ground." □

The master bedroom right and above is connected to the library by double six-panel doors. Brian describes the hunter green and mahogany theme shared by the two rooms as "masculine without being macho." An 18th-century reproduction secretary provides space for antique books and other collections and complements both the color and scale of the canopied bed.

THE ENCHANTING
PURITY OF
WHITE CASTS ITS
SPELL ON AN
ISLAND HOME OFF
CONNECTICUT.

WHITE
Magic

BY MIKE BUTLER

PHOTOGRAPHY BY JON JENSEN
PRODUCED BY BONNIE MAHARAM

Joan Gray doesn't scare easily. If she did, she would have told her husband, Michael, to keep driving the day they first saw the crumbling house and overgrown gardens. She would have bolted after following a path of gold carpeting through a clumsy arrangement of rooms. She never would have taken on the tribulation of a major house renovation. And she never would have left the

safety of her chintz-filled past to try a new kind of traditional style.

The Grays fell for the house, formerly a summer rental haven for film and theater stars, because of its island location off the coast of Connecticut.

After the dust from the remodeling cleared, light poured through dozens of new windows and brought with it a panorama of pastels: the bright pink of sun-

rise, the brilliant blue of midday, the warm apricot of sunset. "Even on days that are not sunny, the quality of light is truly extraordinary," Joan says.

White, she decided, would capture nature's brushwork and the summer-house style she wanted. "I have had a love affair with white for a long time."

As an interior designer for offices, Joan studies the patterns of light and shadow

◆ ◆ ◆

JOAN GRAY, *OPPOSITE TOP*, BUILT PLENTY OF SHELVES AND LEDGES INTO THE LIVING ROOM *ABOVE* FOR DISPLAY SPACE AND WINDOW SEATS. OUTSIDE, *OPPOSITE BOTTOM*, SHE PRESERVED THE 80-YEAR-OLD HOME'S ARTS-AND-CRAFTS ARCHITECTURE.

hite used to be the "I can't decide" color. Now it's the color of choice in traditional rooms whenever simplicity is desired. To pick the white that's right for your home, experiment with several shades. Then watch how they change as light and shadow fall on them during the course of a day.

♦ ♦ ♦

IN THE LIVING ROOM *RIGHT*, THE FIREPLACE PROVIDES AN UNDERSTATED FOCAL POINT. JOAN THOUGHT ABOUT REDOING IT IN STONE BUT GREW TO LOVE THE QUIETNESS OF THE ORIGINAL MANTEL INSTEAD. THE KITCHEN *ABOVE* WAS DIFFICULT TO PLAN BECAUSE WINDOWS LINED MOST OF THE FOUR WALLS. JOAN CUT THE LARGE AREA DOWN TO SIZE WITH A CENTER ISLAND.

If you've been searching for a way to make a room look dressy but not stuffy, try a white-on-white scheme. Forms and fabrics wedded in white fill a room with freshness and light and create a feeling of relaxed elegance.

◆ ◆ ◆

JOAN BUILT THE DINING ROOM *ABOVE* AND *OPPOSITE* AROUND A MAHOGANY TABLE THAT SHE AND MICHAEL BOUGHT AT AUCTION ABOUT 20 YEARS AGO. THE RETRIEVER-ADORNED TEA SET *TOP* REMINDS THEM OF THEIR DOG, ROSCOE.

in each room before picking the shade of white she thinks will look best in it.

For her own kitchen and master bedroom, Joan chose a milky premixed paint, but it took hours of observation and experimentation to come up with the simple matte white that covers the walls of her living and dining rooms.

"I stood over the painter and we kept adding pigment, making it cooler and

warmer until it really felt right," she says.

Once satisfied with her backgrounds, Joan exiled the floral chintz slipcovers to the attic and re-covered most of her upholstered seating pieces with a cream-colored cotton duck. Lace, linens, or throws provide subtle variations on the white-on-white theme in each room.

Restored wood floors, mellow antiques, and splashes of striped fabric, meanwhile,

*T*o avoid having too much
of a good thing, use whites of varying
intensity for walls and fabrics, and bring
metals and woods to the mix. Textures give a white
room the warmth it needs.

♦ ♦ ♦

Joan turned a sitting area into a
master bathroom but left the
original fireplace *above* where it
was. Gray veining in the white
marble inspired the fabric choice
for the vanity *right*. The
crystal and silver pieces belonged
to Joan's mother and
started Joan's collecting passion.

prevent the monochromatic scheme from
becoming monotonous.

Strange things happened when Joan in-
troduced some of her favorite possessions
to this new environment. Some brass
pieces, for instance, fairly screamed, and
the china figurines didn't look right at all.
On the other hand, the Grays' collection
of crystal, silver, pottery, and 19th-
century American art never looked better.

In the beginning, Joan wanted to create the feeling of an elegant, English country lodge minus the color and pattern. She may have done her job too well.

On summer weekends, friends of Michael and Joan and their teenage sons, Benjy and Peter, often fill the Gray lodge to capacity. They spend their days boating and wind surfing, or just watching the egrets, herons, and horseshoe crabs. At night, the Grays and their guests might gather on the beach for a clambake or around a telescope for stargazing. Bathing suits and sarongs are as dressy as it gets.

Joan doesn't scare easily. Unless, maybe, she is confronted by excessive formality. "I had really thought I wanted a Georgian home," she says, "but they felt too prissy to me. This house isn't meant to be taken that seriously." ☐

♦ ♦ ♦

IN THE GRAYS' MASTER BEDROOM
ABOVE, AN EXPANSE OF WHITE
WALLS AND LINENS CREATES A FEELING
OF SERENITY. A PRIMITIVE WOODEN
CHEST, VICTORIAN IRON GARDEN
SEAT, AND OTHER ANTIQUES PROVIDE
TOUCHES OF WARMTH.

𝒯om Page, below, shares a moment with Omar, one of his four dogs. With an artful mix of English and European antiques and Eastern artifacts, the living room right has a rich, layered look inspired by the homes of Edwardian England.

BY DAN WEEKS

PHOTOGRAPHY BY JENIFER JORDAN
PRODUCED BY AMY MUZZY MALIN

Living The EDWARDIAN LIFE

The Dallas home of antiques dealer Tom Page is a tribute to the Edwardian philosophy of eclectic accumulation. Rooms rich with character reflect a long love affair with traveling and collecting.

If you were to tell Tom Page that you liked his decorating scheme, he might not be offended, but he certainly would feel misunderstood. "I don't believe in decorating," says the Dallas antiques dealer. "My philosophy is Edwardian: I believe that rooms should evolve."

During the Edwardian era—about 1880 to 1920—the British empire was at its height. At that time the English upper class—from whose descendants Tom buys much of the 18th- and 19th-century pieces that he owns and sells—traveled widely in the empire's colonies. They developed broad interests and a good eye for both aesthetic value and quality workmanship.

Wherever they went, they bought what they liked and brought cratefuls of their finds back with them. Chinese porcelain, Indian sculptures, and Egyptian archaeological pieces mixed comfortably in their homes with English and continental antiques. In that stable, acquisitive society of titles and grand houses, each generation added its own layer of treasures to the mix until each room became a family history.

"Most people are used to a decorated American look," explains Tom. "If you have a green sofa, you have to have a painting with green in it on the wall. But I like the depth, the history, and the personality of an eclectic look."

Tom loves to mix elements from different periods and cultures. An ivory horse and camel from the collection of the Maharaja of Jaipur, an Egyptian mummy mask, and a contemporary painting share a living room corner, left. *The master bedroom,* below, *is a mix of the exotic (African figures and Indian accessories) and the comfortable (deeply pillowed sofa, leather wing chair, and English pub fender). All balance and symmetry, the house's straightforward exterior,* bottom, *masks its varied contents.*

Edwardian eclecticism can't be bought in large lots. But Tom's home is proof that you needn't inherit a furnished manor to achieve it. When Tom graduated from college, a friend advised him to buy antiques rather than new or reproduction pieces, and to take a long view. As chance would have it, he spent his first year out of college working for an antiques show while looking for a job in finance. "For years I lived with end tables made of shipping crates," he remembers. "As I found pieces that I liked and could afford, I bought them. I preferred to live with makeshift furniture with style rather than buy new pieces." Patience, a lively interest in traveling and antiques, and a good eye slowly transformed his home into a showplace.

As time went on, Tom found he enjoyed living the Edwardian life as much as he did owning the antiques. He left a banking career, purchased Heirloom House Antiques with partner Todd Edmondson, and now spends his time traveling and buying for a clientele that shares his adventurous taste. "I couldn't get the pieces I do buying from others in the business," he explains. "I spend a lot of time in people's houses in England, for instance, where dealings are all very personal. I go to the source."

Like his intrepid Edwardian predecessors, Tom believes in research and in developing one's expertise. He also retains an

*The ram's head on an African Awari
game board guards antique French dinner plates, a
Victorian butter dish, and contemporary service
plates on Tom's dining room table, **right**. The table itself is
a sheet of glass atop a 16th- or 17th-century
architectural capital that Tom found in a field in India.
French art nouveau dining room chairs, **below**,
feature their original faux-tortoiseshell finish and art
nouveau fabric.*

Edwardian inquisitiveness, and a willingness to be swayed by emotion. Although he specializes in 18th- and 19th-century antiques, Tom owns two art deco wing chairs, paintings by contemporary artists, some pre-Christian-era artifacts, and a good deal of primitive art. Ultimately, what much of the stuff has in common is that Tom Page has collected it.

And that, Tom believes, is enough—if the collector has a good eye, has done his homework, and has the confidence to live in a home that reflects his passions and eccentricities more than it does conventions of style, period, or design. "I've never bought anything knowing where I wanted to put it," says Tom. "When I'm on a buying trip with my antique-store clients, I tell them, 'Buy what you

> *I've never bought
> anything knowing where I
> wanted to put it. . . . Buy
> what you like.*
>
> ────── TOM PAGE

like. Buy what's good. We will find a place for it.' "

The proof of this theory is in Tom's home, which is a rich pudding indeed. "It's constantly changing," he says. "After returning from India, it takes on an Indian look. If I've just been to Egypt, the Egyptian feeling is strongest. When the shipping crates arrive after each trip, I walk around the house with things, looking for the right place to put them. It is sort of doing archaeology in reverse: Each piece reminds me of somewhere I've been, someone I've met."

It is sort of like doing archaeology in reverse: Each piece reminds me of somewhere I've been.

—— TOM PAGE

In spite of the great value and age of some of the pieces in his collection and their freight of priceless associations, Tom's house is not a museum. Four dogs romp freely with Tom's teenage son on the fine Bijar rug, and two cats lounge on the 17th-century French tapestry pillows. "Edwardian houses were meant to be lived in," he says. "I've never been married to my possessions. Stuff is stuff. If I was intimidated by my collection, I wouldn't enjoy having it around." □

Hand-blocked wallpaper, a Japanese vase, Indian carvings, African sculpture, and a contemporary table offer an eclectic greeting from the front hall above.

Black-and-white tile with black grouting, slate-look flooring, plantation shutters, and old glass-front cabinets give the remodeled kitchen left *country charm. The room provides a clean, graphic backdrop to more of Tom's treasured collectibles, including an 18th-century French table and 18th-century English oak chairs with rush seats.*

April

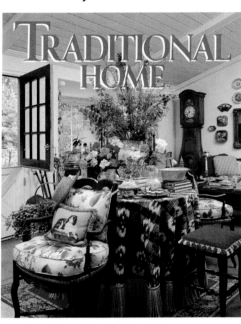

TRADITIONAL HOME

Interior designer Charles Faudree's shingle-style house in Tulsa holds decorating surprises in every room.

ENDLESS WONDER

BY PAMELA J. WILSON

PHOTOGRAPHY BY GENE JOHNSON • PRODUCED BY NANCY E. INGRAM
FLORAL DESIGNS BY MARY MURRAY FLOWERS

Having moved five times in the past 10 years, interior designer Charles Faudree admits to being fickle when it comes to houses. "I feel about my houses the same way Elizabeth Taylor feels about her husbands: Each one is my best and my last," he says with a grin.

Speaking of his latest acquisition and remodel—a delightful Dutch colonial built in 1923—Charles, a man who thrives on change, insists that this *really* is his all-time favorite house, and that he has no intention of moving . . . well, not for at least 10 years.

Located in the heart of Tulsa, on a lovely tree-shaded street, the house *above* beckoned to Charles long before he purchased it in 1989. "I had always admired this dwelling," he says. "It has so much architectural charm."

Make no bones about it, Charles is a dog fancier from way back. Members of his endearing canine collection range from the porcelain bulldog and the needlepoint spaniels in the sun-room vignette, right, *to the three lovable pooches posing on their master's lap,* left.

The sun-room features a romantic mix of country French furnishings, delightful fabrics in florals and plaids, and, of course, an intriguing array of collections. What looks like a tile floor is actually concrete, scored and stained a rich terra-cotta.

I FEEL ABOUT MY HOUSES THE SAME WAY
ELIZABETH TAYLOR FEELS ABOUT HER HUSBANDS:
EACH ONE IS MY BEST AND MY LAST.

—— CHARLES FAUDREE

The living room below combines English elegance and French élan. The rich paneled walls are British in feeling, but the furnishings—including the antique commode, the wine table, the chinoiserie side table, and the Bergère and fauteuil chairs—are trés French.

Presided over by an imposing buffet à deux corps, the dining room above, with its antique French farm table and candlelit chandelier, is a treat to behold. One of Charles' first acquisitions—an antique tole footbath—has a place of honor beneath the French Empire convex mirror. Twin lamps on both sides of the mirror were fashioned from Italian wooden candlesticks.

From streetside it's a rare passerby who isn't beguiled by the front gabled roof, the shuttered crank-out windows, and the window boxes brimming with ferns and begonias.

If the exterior of the house entices, the interior enthralls. Here is where Charles, with his passion for "all things beautiful," really shines.

Visitors to the house are always intrigued, and sometimes awed, by what they find inside. Each room (there are nine in all) is a feast for the eyes. Along with a prodigious quantity of museum-quality furniture, artwork, glorious fabrics, and magnificent rugs, there are collections—and more collections—everywhere.

Charles, you see, can't be contained—at least not when it comes to collecting. The objects of his affection include (but certainly aren't limited to) dog statuary and other canine-related items, antique porcelain plates and tureens, antique tapestries and paisley shawls, antique tortoiseshell, birdcages, leather-bound books, Napoleonic treasures, and needlepoint pillows—many of which he makes himself. He also has a soft

Any surface—table, shelf, mantel, or ledge—is a candidate for Charles' magical touch. Here he has embellished his baby grand piano with a prized collection of antique tortoiseshell. Placed in concert, the small items pique the interest of all who pass by.

*Devotee of dogs that he is, Charles has embellished the ultra-inviting English-style library **above** with numerous examples from his large and lovable canine collection. Many breeds are represented, in mediums ranging from oil paintings to bronze, porcelain, silver, and terra-cotta statuary—and all are displayed with distinction.*

spot for Staffordshire—castles, cottages, chickens, and cows.

Collecting, for Charles, is more than a personal pleasure, it's a professional one as well. He travels extensively, here and abroad, searching for antiques and other treasures that will please his clients and fill the shelves of his Tulsa antiques shop.

Amazingly, though the house is filled with an abundance of wonderful things, there's nothing *de trop* about the overall effect. Quite the opposite. Though Charles indulges his rooms, he doesn't sate them. Like a master chef using delectable yet potent spices and herbs, he knows instinctively just when to stop. Moreover, he knows when to continue. There's no such thing as a finished room, not in Charles' mind. Perfection, for him, is an ongoing process, one that involves endless trial and error. "The only perfection is change," he insists.

So change-oriented is Charles that when he moved into his present house, he started almost from scratch. (Many of the collections and some of the antique furnishings made the move from his previous home, but *all* of the upholstery and drapery fabrics are new.) Most amazingly, it took a mere six months to create the "lived-in-forever" look you see pictured here—the kind of look that takes most mortals years, if not a lifetime, to attain.

Busy as he is with his own house, his clients, and his shop, Charles manages to find time to enjoy the fruits of his labors. "I think the busier a person is, the more home means," he says, adding, "I personally love to be home surrounded by the things I love." And what things and what rooms does Charles love the most? He can't be pinned down, not exactly. "I live throughout the house, not every day, but by the end of the week, every room will have been lived in for one occasion or another," he says.

*The library window **right,** with views of the terrace beyond, is furnished, Faudree-style, to perfection. Serving as a centerpiece for the intimate grouping is an antique French red lacquer tea table, topped with a porcelain pug-turned-lamp. Note the stack of books used as a table.*

40

All kinds of enticements, visual and victual, await in the kitchen. To be savored is the French farmhouse ambience, enhanced by collections of Staffordshire cows, left, and assorted nesting chickens—some of which can be seen roosting in and upon the antique "thing" hanging over the island counter above. Charles, left, isn't sure what the "thing" is, but knows he likes it.

◆

With its own bath and direct access to the outdoor pool, the downstairs guest room below is a favorite of visitors. Equally appreciated—and admired—is the iron sleigh bed, topped with needlepoint dog pillows and an interloping cat.

*I*t *is here,* **right,** *where Charles retreats at the end of a hectic day. Waiting to soothe him is a restful color scheme; rich, room-darkening velvet draperies; and all the accoutrements needed for peaceful pursuits and sleeping comfort. Charles (and his dogs) are particularly fond of this room because it has a private staircase leading to late-night snacks in the kitchen.*

Though he doesn't play favorites as far as rooms are concerned, he's unequivocal when it comes to color. "Red is my favorite color," Charles pronounces. "Every house should have at least one red room."

In his house it's the library, pictured on *pages 40 and 41.* Beautifully embraced by Persian red walls, a warming fireplace, and bookshelves laden with leather-bound tomes, this is the kind of room Anglophiles dream of. Charles is willing to admit that this is his favorite room, at least part of the year. "From November to January, this is where you're most apt to find me," he says. And no wonder. Furnished

*T*rue *to the French Empire period, Napoleon reigns in the master bath below. The "Little General" was the focus of Charles' first foray into the world of collecting, and it is here where much of the accrued memorabilia is now stylishly housed.*

as it is in the luxurious comfort of an English gentlemen's club, only a diehard ascetic could resist the room's compelling allure.

Speaking of comfort, as a professional designer, Charles makes it a point to advise his clients that a room isn't elegant unless it's also inviting. "There's no reason why you can't have both beauty and comfort," he insists.

There's no question that Charles follows his own advice. There's not a room in his house that doesn't combine comfort with eye appeal. "There's no hands-off policy here," he says. And indeed there's not. The entire house is designed to be fully enjoyed—to make Charles, and all comers, feel relaxed, at ease, at home. Sofas and chairs, all covered in fine, even exquisite, fabrics are meant to be sat on, not just admired from afar. Similarly, collections and *objets:* Whether priceless in real or sentimental value, none are off-limits to touch.

O*pen to the elements on one side, the "outdoor" room **right** nonetheless affords year-round living enjoyment. Casual wicker seating pieces and a country French table and chairs are perfect accompaniments for alfresco entertaining. The fireplace saves the day when it's cool; the stone floor makes no mind of bathers who come in, dripping wet, from the pool.*

One of the most inviting rooms in the house is not really a room per se, but a ceilinged three-walled space, *right,* that opens directly to the garden and a lovely outdoor swimming pool. Though exposed on one side to the elements, the room, with its large stone fireplace, is fully functional most of the year. Charles spends a lot of time here, whether alone reading or entertaining—something he loves to do, and quite often.

Guests love to join Charles when he's working in the kitchen. Understandably. He's a charming host, a great conversationalist, and, rumor has it, a terrific cook. Moreover, the kitchen itself (see *pages 68–69*) is a conversation piece. Styled in the mien of a country French farmhouse, the room holds all kinds of pleasures, culinary and otherwise.

For starters, there's the enchanting collection of Staffordshire chickens and cows, artfully arranged and displayed, en masse, to perfection. Then there are the details,

the clever touches and surprise elements that, according to master detailer Charles, "make all the difference between a so-so room and one that's truly spectacular." Note, for example, the kitchen ceiling—far from ordinary and wonderfully apropos for the country French scheme. It is composed of beams with grape-stake fencing running between them. The fencing, by the way, was salvaged from Charles' backyard, hosed down at high pressure, whitewashed, then cut to fit between the beams.

Yet another pleasing detail in the kitchen is the faux-stone wallpaper, complete with a "chiseled" (actually painted) keystone of the date Charles moved into the house. "I love to make my mark," he says with a smile. And in an endless variety of wonderful and fascinating ways, he most certainly has. □

I
ALWAYS TELL MY CLIENTS THAT "DETAIL IS IT."
WHETHER IT'S FRINGE ON A SOFA OR FRUIT IN A BOWL,
IT'S THE DETAILS THAT MAKE A ROOM SPECIAL.

—— CHARLES FAUDREE

PEACEFUL
COEXISTENCE

Tʜᴇ LIVING ROOM *RIGHT*
EXHIBITS NEAL'S FLAIR FOR
JUXTAPOSITION.
AFRICAN BOXES, A THREE-
TIERED WHATNOT, AND A
CONTEMPORARY SOFA
COMFORTABLY COMMINGLE.

*Dallas designer Neal Stewart blends contemporary
and traditional modes with deceptive ease. His secret?
Each piece he owns delivers high-impact style.*

BY CARLA BREER HOWARD

PHOTOGRAPHY BY JENIFER JORDAN • PRODUCED BY AMY MUZZY MALIN

NEAL STEWART, *ABOVE,*
SPORTS HIS CURRENT
FAVORITE ACCENT COLOR, A
VIVID CHINESE YELLOW,
IN THE ENTRY OF HIS
DALLAS TOWN HOUSE.

49

With a gentle accent bespeaking his northern Louisiana origin, interior designer Neal Stewart characterizes his style as contemporary. To the extent that his rooms show an aversion to clutter, a pleasure in recurring swashes of black, and a preference for bold furnishings and artwork, then, yes, the style is contemporary.

However, Neal also demonstrates a traditional bent, expanding beyond the contemporary mode with the liberal use of antiques and reproductions in his interiors. It is his particular blending of contemporary purity with traditional grace—a sort of bravura eclecticism—that gives Neal's work a personal and fresh point of view.

Neal's Dallas town house exemplifies his approach, achieving a kind of timelessness through a judicious mix of the artifacts of many periods and cultures. At the core is an internal selection process that is almost Oriental in its discipline to a central vision. This knowing what to use and precisely how to use it also applies to his stringent editing of accessories and calculated introduction of strong color accents on a pervasive base of black. The result, says Neal, is that "there is nothing in my home that says trendy or postmodern, or alludes to a particular year—even down to the deliberate lack of a fashion color."

Instead, each object or piece stands on its own design strength without needing to be paired or used en suite to achieve impact. The acquisition of furnishings bursting with character is not

THIS VIEW OF THE LIVING ROOM *RIGHT* EXHIBITS THE WARMING EFFECT OF BLACK. A TRADITIONAL CHESTERFIELD SOFA IS CONTEMPORIZED WITH A BLACK-AND-TAUPE-STRIPED FABRIC TRIMMED WITH BLACK ENAMEL NAILHEADS. ON THE TABLE *ABOVE*, ACCESSORIES ARE KEPT TO A MINIMUM.

accidental. Neal consciously seeks out traditional furnishings that offer some unique quality—a kind of boldness. He then takes a piece and builds even more drama by employing unexpected finishing and upholstery choices. Eschewing the conventional leather and brass-tack treatment, for example, Neal covered a classic chesterfield sofa for his living room in a crisp black-and-taupe-striped fabric tacked with black enamel nailheads.

He also exploits the shock value of placing pieces from diverse periods and styles in juxtaposition instead of seeking obvious harmonies. "Often I'll put traditional and clean-lined contemporary pieces together so the wonderful traditional pieces really stand out," he says. The chesterfield sofa, for example, is grouped with a slick black-lacquered Dunbar coffee table accessorized with African boxes, two black all-rubber chairs, and a Diego Giacometti-inspired lamp. Facing off across the fireplace is another intimate seating area composed of a contemporary leather love seat, a traditional English three-tiered whatnot table, and a stately Louis XVI-style side chair.

The effect of this approach is to lead the eye to settle on and explore each element in the room. One's gaze moves from a Chippendale-style stool to a Victorian wicker chair, and then on to the adjacent round faux-marble table and a tortoiseshell-finish mirror shimmering against the brick wall just beyond.

A long-standing admiration for the work of architect Le Cobusier and sculptor Isamu Noguchi is expresssed in Neal's minimalist treatment of decorating accessories and collections. In order to

> O**ften I'll put traditional and clean-lined contemporary pieces together so the wonderful traditional pieces really stand out.**
>
> —— NEAL STEWART

focus on the very best, Neal inspires his clients to reevaluate their possessions and put things away.

A minimalist's passion for black is also expressed in Neal's work. From his earliest days as an interior design major at Louisiana Tech University, he has loved the drama of black. "Black is classic, timeless, and actually works to warm up a space," Neal says. When he first moved into his current home, Neal kept the wood floors bare. Later, he added black sisal area rugs. The result was a new warmth and intimacy. Although his taste for black has been a constant, the colors he chooses to play off the black vary. A deep strong Chinese yellow is his current favorite.

Neal Stewart not only designs residential interiors, he has also done work for several prestigious tabletop manufacturers. He has just completed a five-year project designing all the U.S. and Caribbean stores and showrooms of the quintessentially traditional Waterford/Wedgwood company. Neal's focus is often, therefore, directed to displaying objects to their best advantage—an approach seen in the design for his town home as well. This talent for identifying and presenting the distinctive qualities of each element in a room imbues a timeless classicism and harmony, plus a remarkable individuality to his balanced interiors. □

In the bedroom *right*, the black leather upholstery on the Louis XVI-style bed relates to the nearby contemporary Dunbar chair. The red-lacquer table in the foreground shows the designer's judicious use of vibrant color to punctuate an otherwise muted color scheme. The courtyard *above* offers calm respite among the caladiums and palm trees.

BY MIKE BUTLER
PHOTOGRAPHY BY TOMMY MIYASAKI
PRODUCED BY JOAN DEKTAR

WORLDLY WISE

*Ed and Susie Beall's Pacific Coast
home is a reflection of their
own life-style—adventurous, impulsive,
and full of energy.*

 Whenever Ed and Susie Beall,
top, *return from a trip, their luggage
bulges with books and decorative objects,
many of which have found a home in
the living room* **opposite.** *The sphinx in
front of the window, for instance, came
from a Greek antiques store. Their
Mediterranean-style house,* **above,** *built
in 1927, is characteristic of the Palos
Verdes peninsula in Southern California.*

vacation for Ed Beall means exploring the head-
waters of the Amazon or the wildlife on the
Galápagos Islands. It means running the Paris
marathon or hot-air ballooning in Moscow. When
the energetic architect returns home to Southern California, his
diary includes sketches and notes of interesting eaves and ornamental motifs, as well as of unusual plants and animals. His
scrimshaw, bird-egg, and animal-skull collections grow. In fact,
it's difficult to tell at times whether Ed is a designer or a natural-
ist, says his wife, Susie. "We're quite sure he was Charles Dar-
win in a previous life."

Ed's practice is diverse. He's worked on everything from a
Marine Corps dining room to an Aspen ski resort. Not surprisingly, the Bealls practice an adventurous, eclectic decorating
style in their own Palos Verdes home, an architectural standout
in an area known for Mediterranean-style villas. "We fell in love
with it without even seeing the inside," Susie says.

A good thing, because the inside of the long-neglected home was a disaster. Remodeling involved repairing water damage, adding a few windows, and tearing down ceilings. A utility room was combined with the original kitchen to gain an open, efficient space with views toward the garden. Ed and Susie relied on some talented craftspeople, but the Bealls and their four sons worked right alongside.

An interior designer, Susie sponge-painted walls throughout the house and executed the faux-tortoiseshell finish in Ed's dressing room and the crackle finish in the kitchen.

When traveling, she takes pictures of paint finishes, ornamentation, and natural materials and files them for reference. The walls in the living room and master bedroom resemble limestone she once saw in France.

"Being an interior designer is difficult because you're not in control of so many aspects," Susie says. "If you order a piece of furniture, the vendor might tell you it's back-ordered, and you get frustrated. I think that's why I love to do the faux finishes and painting so much. I'm in absolute control. If something is wrong, I can fix it personally."

A case in point is the new plaster fireplace mantel in the living room. "I painted it to look like dark green granite. After about six months, I couldn't stand it," Susie says. "For about half an hour, it looked like travertine, but that was too busy. Finally, I just antiqued it."

Once satisifed with her backgrounds, Susie painted curtain rods and chose linen draperies

Filled with light and garden views, the small morning room below, adjacent to the living room, is easily arranged for breakfast, a light lunch, or tea in the afternoon. Ed lassoed the eye-catching papier-mâché burro during a trip to Mexico.

Reproduction settees and cane chairs pull up around a contemporary lacquer table to form an intimate conversation area in the living room above. Ed's interest in collecting scrimshaw (carved whale bones), evident throughout the living room, grew while designing a development with a whaling motif on Maui.

I LOVE TO DO FAUX FINISHES BECAUSE I'M
IN ABSOLUTE CONTROL. IF SOMETHING IS WRONG, I
CAN FIX IT PERSONALLY.

—— SUSIE BEALL

Although the kitchen was completely remodeled into an efficient galley design, vintage light fixtures and other architectural elements, such as the large arched window **opposite,** *are in keeping with the house. Mexican and European earthenware, baskets, and other dinnerware are easily reached via a library ladder. Ed took the lead role in fashioning the mosaic work* **above;** *Susie deserves credit for the crackle finishes on the cabinets. Some of the finest specimens in Ed's quirky bird-egg collection come home to roost in the dining room* **below.**

to match. That way, similar to a museum, the undistracted eye can focus on the furnishings and Ed's collections.

"Ed had always wanted to live in a museum," Susie jokes. "It's really fun to show people the things that are in the house."

Susie and Ed also had fun doing the mosaic mural above the range and oven in the kitchen. "I wanted the design to look like a mosaic fragment," Ed explains. "I got the idea from a mural in a villa in Pompeii."

Susie says the mural wound up being more of a fragment than they had planned. "We determined that it took about six hours to do a square foot," she says. "After a couple of weeks, we ended up painting most of it in."

While lying on their backs on scaffolding, Ed and son James painstakingly tiled the kitchen ceiling. James was in bed next to the kitchen that night when he heard the horrifying sound of tiles plopping to the floor. Fortunately, only a few fell out, and Ed left it the way it was: "I think it enhances the antique look a bit to have a small tile missing here and there." Now, he likes to tell guests how he discovered this fantastic mosaic ceiling after he took out the acoustic tiles.

In less than six months, the inside was finished, and the Bealls turned their attention to the garden.

"There was a huge pine tree growing straight

Painted surfaces that resemble tortoiseshell in Ed's dressing room **below** *are another tribute to Susie's artistry with a brush. Built-in cabinets provide plenty of storage, and closets lurk behind the mirror-face doors.*

Susie combined two twin-size panels from an antiques store in San Juan Capistrano to make the distinctive headboard in the master bedroom **above.** *The terra-cotta plaques on display in the niche came from an antiques store in Greece. They once decorated the rooflines of old buildings there.*

ED HAD ALWAYS WANTED TO LIVE IN
A MUSEUM. IT'S REALLY FUN TO SHOW PEOPLE THE
THINGS THAT ARE IN THE HOUSE.

—— SUSIE BEALL

Although the dimensions of the master bedroom **right** *didn't change with remodeling, Ed's design for the new fireplace and plank ceiling with big trusses of resawn wood dramatically improved its appearance and comfort level.*

The addition of new closets in the guest bedroom **below** *compensated for a lack of storage and formed the frame for another arched window, softened with the addition of a little sheer fabric and a cherub. The view is toward a steep, secluded slope of the garden.*

A moiré taffeta skirt, finished with bows, adorns Susie's dressing table above, located in the guest room. Silver and pearl accessories and an array of papier-mâché dolls further feminize the area.

up out of the center, which put the whole garden in shadow," according to Susie. "Once all the shadow was gone, we could see how awful everything was."

In addition to clearing away trees and brush, the original terraces that tamed the steep slope had to be shored up.

"The poor kids," Susie says. "Every time they came home there would be pallets of stone or a lot of plants on the driveway. They'd walk in saying, 'Top terrace, right?' Without the boys we never could have done it."

Ed designed the gazebo at the top of the garden, which Susie calls the "Far Pavilion," and the arbor that marks the entrance to the "Puerto Vallarta" terrace.

Landscape designer Julie Heinsheimer, who works in Ed's office, helped the Bealls pick hardy old roses, succulents, bougainvillea, palms, and other tropical plants that would thrive in their climate. "She keeps me out of trouble when I go to the nursery," Susie says. "I have a hard time telling a geranium from a weed. I may not know anything about the garden, but I enjoy it."

More time was spent on the fish grotto than anything else, according to Susie. The pool leaked at first. Then, the night after they had stocked the pond, a family of raccoons helped

The Bealls devoted one portion of their terraced backyard to old rose varieties, **right.** *Remaining terraces are devoted to culinary herbs, Oriental-style plants, and other special plant collections. Old overgrown trees that had cast the entire garden in shade were removed before replanting could begin.*

Calling it the "Far Pavilion," **above,** *the Bealls planted this gazebo on the garden's highest spot. The steep climb is rewarded with spectacular views of the ocean and sunsets.*

themselves to a dinner of koi, a prized and expensive variety of Japanese carp. Now, an electric wire strung around the pond protects the fish, but the raccoons don't exactly appreciate that solution. "They get mad and rip up the garden in front of it," Susie says. "I plant things there every other week."

Whenever the raccoons or work at the office really gets her down, all Susie has to do is go to her dressing table and reach for one of the papier-mâché dolls she has lined up there—presents from Ed a few Christmases ago.

"It seems like we're just surrounded by people all the time," Susie explains. "All I wanted to do one year was go away. Ed always gives me something really neat for Christmas, and I couldn't figure out why he had given me twelve papier-mâché dolls: He'd slit open the back of each one and stuffed a vacation in it. Whenever I want to go away, I just surrender a doll. I think I have eight of them left." □

June

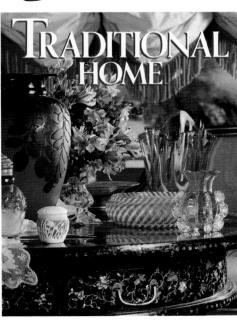

Designed with comfort and hospitality in mind, the new Memphis home of George and Marcia Bryan is a beautiful blend of time-honored style and Southern tradition.

A Home for All Reasons

BY PAMELA J. WILSON

PRODUCED BY MARY ANNE THOMSON • PHOTOGRAPHY BY HOPKINS ASSOCIATES

House-wise, the Bryans have the best of all worlds. Their new eight-sided residence, above, beautifully accommodates large social gatherings and serves as an intimate family home. The couple's favorite retreat is a cocoonlike study, left, located within the master suite. Adding greatly to the room's richness and warmth is the claret-color wallpaper, an American documentary wood-block print.

69

An enticing indoor swimming pool is the core of the house and the centerpiece around which the Bryans and their many social functions revolve. Propped with garden benches and chairs, lots of greenery, and Victorian Era Grecian urns, the pool calls to mind an elegant English conservatory. Adding to the pool's great allure is the fact it can be seen and admired from every room on the ground floor. A special air system keeps the smell of chlorine at bay.

Though its public face is formal and, some might say, imposing, the Memphis home of George and Marcia Bryan is wonderfully friendly inside. Every room in the part-Federal, part-Georgian structure is designed to please—not just the Bryans and their four college-age children, but guests as well.

Guests come often and usually in large numbers. George is an executive with a nationally known corporation and, in this capacity, entertains frequently. Both Bryans are also active community leaders and are frequently called upon to host civic functions and other social affairs.

When they decided to custom-build a house in 1987, they were faced with a dilemma. "We knew we needed a big house for entertainment purposes, but we also wanted an intimate family house, a place where we'd feel comfortable on a daily basis," Marcia explains. "We weren't sure we could do both."

Architect Charles Shipp came up with an ideal solution: a 5,550-square-foot, octagonal-shape house with a fabulous sky-lit indoor swimming pool as the focal point.

The pool, in more ways than one, is the hub of the home. Not only does the house wrap around it (there's a view of water from every room on the ground floor), it plays a central role in the Bryans' lives. "It's a real crowd pleaser," says Marcia. "The kids use it primarily for swimming parties, but for us, it's a natural extension of the house." And thanks to a special air system that eliminates chlorine odors and saunalike humidity, the pool is a year-round interior habitat, not a place apart.

A Home for All Reasons

🐦 *Reminiscent of a turret in a castle, the octagon-shape entry* right *mimics the shape of the house. Adding a touch of tongue-in-cheek is a reproduction 18th-century wood-block wallpaper, designed to look like stone. Floors here, as in the rest of the house, are 8-inch heart pine, coated with polyurethane for easy maintenance.*

*W*armly embraced by pumpkin-color walls, the Bryans' dining room **left**
holds a promise of pleasures—culinary and companionable. A magnificent Adams-style
silver-leaf mirror reflects the room's ambrosial ambience and accentuates
the shimmer and sparkle of fine crystal and candlelight.

*W*hether they're home alone or hosting a party, the Bryans spend a lot of time
in the great-room **below**. Encircled by a balcony and topped with a skylight, the room
has an atriumlike atmosphere, heightened by the proximity of the pool. The table
above is one of many wood pieces handcrafted by Eldred Wheeler of Massachusetts.

A friendly kind of formality pervades the parlor right. *Located just off the foyer, the room connects—via pocket doors—to the great-room. The focal point is a handsome colonial Revival fireplace with a broken-arch pediment and gesso decoration. Lamps on the mantel are converted Sheffield candlesticks.*

 A lovely tiger-maple secretary, below, *is vitalized by the presence of mementos, many of which were found by Marcia when accompanying George on his business travels.*

Conveniently entered through the great-room, the master bedroom, and an enclosed brick patio, the pool area—with its English conservatory ambience—is a Marcia-pleaser, too. "I never imagined how much I'd enjoy having an indoor pool. It's just wonderful to be anywhere in the house and be able to gaze at water. I find it a very soothing presence," she says.

The rooms that embrace the pool—entryway, parlor, great-room, master suite, kitchen, and dining room—also connect to each other.

"The house flows beautifully," says Steven Bengel, the Memphis interior designer who helped shape the decorative personality of the Bryan home. Working closely with George and Marcia and architect Shipp from the beginning, Bengel created an adaptable environment—one that is formal enough to accommodate the Bryans' elegant business and social events yet is fully functional and geared to family living.

The parlor shown at *right* is the most formal room in the house, but it is far from fusty. Furnishings, though refined in character, are wonderfully comfortable and thoughtfully arranged to promote

A Home for All Reasons

sociability. Walls, painted robin's-egg blue, add to the affable ambience.

The most casual room in the house—the great-room (*page* 73)—features French doors on both sides of the fireplace that open to the pool area. When they're home from college, the Bryans' four children and their friends commandeer this room as their headquarters. Understandably. Not only is a "swimming hole" in close proximity, but a private staircase leads directly to their bedrooms.

When Marcia and George wish to get away from the goings-on, they find respite in their master suite *right*. More than mere sleeping quarters, the expansive suite includes an exercise room, a sybaritic bath, and a peaceful, put-your-feet-up study. So appealing is the suite that when the Bryans have parties, they open it up to guests.

When asked what she likes most about the house, Marcia was quick to reply. "That's easy. It pampers us as a family and pleases our guests. We feel we have the best of all worlds." □

*D*esign inspiration for the master bath above *came from the magnificent Art Nouveau cameo mirror. The rest of the wood cabinetry and trim was faux-grained to match the French quartersawed oak. The red marble countertop and floor contribute to the room's rich glow.*

A Home for All Reasons

*T*eamed with a Regency chair from Edinburgh, the mahogany desk* left *is used by Marcia for paying bills. The lamps—converted candlesticks— once belonged to Marcia's mother.*

There's more than meets the eye in the Bryans' spacious and gracious master bedroom suite. Connected to the romantically endowed sleeping/sitting area above is a cozy English-style study, a fully equipped exercise room, a luxurious bath, and a private, walled-in patio. And that's not all. The room, furnished with chintz-covered easy chairs, a cherry four-poster, and a heavenly blue-painted tray ceiling, has its own access to the indoor pool. Note the bedspread: It's made of antique lace curtain panels, sewn together.

SCHOOLED IN
TRADITION

Memphis residents Carol and Walter Ruck have infused their former one-room schoolhouse with charm, tradition, and true Southern style.

No one's quite sure when the venerable schoolhouse was built, but carpenters who worked on the remodel and renovation uncovered clues that suggest the structure is at least 150 years old. One clue—an old cistern—was salvaged by Carol and given new life as an outdoor planter.

BY PAMELA J. WILSON

•

PRODUCED BY MARY ANNE THOMSON

PHOTOGRAPHY BY HOPKINS ASSOCIATES

Feminine but not frilly, elegant but not ostentatious, the living room below is a reflection of Carol's worldly tastes. Gathered in gracious harmony are a Hepplewhite sofa, a brocade Louis XIV chair, an Adam-style satinwood chair, and an English Georgian coffee table—all beautifully anchored by a Portuguese needlepoint rug. An Italian Renaissance table, left, holds assorted treasures, among them a pair of lamps made from English Victorian mantel ornaments. A painted Art Deco screen serves as an imposing backdrop.

welve years ago, Carol Ruck met and promptly fell in love with the house of her dreams—an early 19th-century, one-room schoolhouse in Memphis. Even though the house was nothing more than an empty shell (the interior had been gutted), Carol was smitten with the structure and jumped at the chance to buy it. "What captivated me was the architecture," she says. "I've always loved old houses, and this one was not only quite old but looked like a storybook cottage." And to Carol's mind, the gutted interior was an asset, not a drawback. "With no interior walls to worry about, I was able to dictate the new floor plan, to essentially build a 'new' house within an old one," she says.

Working with a contractor, Carol, who was single at the time, proceeded to remodel the schoolhouse to her liking. This involved, among other things, lowering the 15-foot ceilings to 11½ feet, installing new plumbing and wiring, converting the coal-burning fireplaces to wood-burning, and, of course, creating rooms where none had been before.

The result was a charming, albeit small, five-room house, consisting of a living room, dining room, kitchen, one bedroom,

Designer Steven Bengel, in addition to helping the Rucks incorporate their possessions, assisted in finding accessories. When it came to lamps, the couple didn't have to look far: One of Bengel's fortes is turning old candlesticks and vases into lovely light fixtures. Examples include the lamps on the mantel left and those on the table in the entry below. Right: A still life of heirlooms silhouetted against an antique lace curtain.

and den. Carol was thrilled with her Lilliputian abode. "After all," she explains, "I was living alone then and didn't want or need very much space."

Little did she know that Kismet was waiting in the wings. Indeed, no sooner had she fully ensconced herself in her new surroundings than she met—and promptly fell in love with—the man of her dreams, Walter Ruck. When the subject of marriage came up, so, naturally, did the question of where they would live. Not surprisingly, Carol made a strong pitch for her beloved schoolhouse, and Walter—an agreeable husband-to-be—acquiesced.

As anyone who has ever combined households is aware, the process isn't always easy. Tastes differ (he loves country, she adores sleek contemporary); color schemes clash (she has a

Ranking as one of Carol's most prized possessions is this 1840s English Regency mahogany drop-front desk, **left.** *On display is a cherished collection of Victorian silver miniatures, many of which are mementos from Carol and Walter's travels abroad.*

Of great sentimental value is the framed child's wedding costume, **right.** *Worn by Carol's late father when he was 5 years old, the exquisite, hand-embroidered satin heirloom was a gift to Carol from her mother. The table is English satinwood.*

When my daddy was five years old, he wore this embroidered satin outfit in a wedding. After he died, my mother had the costume beautifully framed and gave it to me. I love it.

—— CAROL RUCK

penchant for soft pastels, he likes anything as long as it's brown). Then there's the matter of logistics: How does one fit another's belongings into one's already-furnished house?

As luck would have it, Carol and Walter faced few of these niggling newlywed problems. "It's amazing how our furniture fit," she says. "What I needed, he had, and vice versa. Our only duplicates were king-size beds." Best of all, the couple found they were completely compatible in matters of taste. "We always see eye-to-eye, even when it comes to collecting art."

There was one difficulty to which Carol admits, however. "When Walter first moved in, I was unwilling to give up any of my closet space to make room for his clothes," she confesses sheepishly. Needless to say, Walter was far from satisfied with this no-closet arrangement, and sought immediate remedy in the form of a new addition.

"Actually, the original plan called for nothing more than a spacious new closet," explains Carol. "Somehow, though, it evolved into a new bath and dressing area for him, plus a separate sitting area with a fireplace and doors leading to an enclosed brick courtyard. Now, he has more closet space than I do," she laughs, "but together we have a fabulous round-the-clock room that we both fully enjoy."

The lovely bedroom addition (*pages 88-89*) is but one of two projects the Rucks have completed since they merged lives and households in 1983. The other—a sun-room designed to

A new sun-room addition did wonders to open the Rucks' galley-style kitchen, **left**. *The counter, renewed with mauve and lavender-tone tile, divides the spaces without obstructing the view.*

*D*esigned to look like an enclosed porch, the sun-room **below** *features a beaded ceiling and an old brick floor. Furnished with 1920s-vintage wicker, the sun-room is a favorite gathering place of the Rucks and their friends.* **Right:** *A collection of Staffordshire on display.*

look like an enclosed summer porch—is connected to the galley-style kitchen *left* and *above*. The couple, and their Doberman pinscher Faith, are drawn to the sun-room like magnets. "We practically live in here," says Carol. "It's the perfect place for reading the paper, sipping morning coffee, perusing the mail, paying bills, or just relaxing." It's also a popular place when the couple entertain. Both Rucks are gourmet cooks, so dinner guests tend to gravitate here to nibble hors d'oeuvres and chat with the resident chefs.

Dinners are served in the elegantly appointed dining room, complete with its own warming fireplace and original heart-pine floors. Located just off the foyer, this room, like the living room,

Designed to cater to creature comforts, the Rucks' remodeled bedroom, **below** *and* **right,** *is a serene, restful retreat. Amenities include a pleasant sitting area, complete with a fireplace, a dressing room, and doors leading to a private courtyard. Reigning with authority at the foot of the linen-bedecked bed is an English mahogany chest of drawers, topped with a Regency burled walnut shaving mirror and a pair of Art Nouveau lamps. The French Victorian love seat* **right** *holds special meaning for Carol: The needlepoint was done by her mother.*

W̶alter and I love the timeless elegance of formal, traditional furnishings, but only in settings where the mood is relaxed.

—— CAROL RUCK

is formally furnished but far from straitlaced. The Rucks—in their eight years of marriage, remodeling, and decorating—have done everything possible to make their home a gracious, welcoming one. "Walter and I love the beauty and elegance of formal furnishings, but only in a relaxed, comfortable context. When we entertain, we treat our guests to the best of everything—fine china, sterling silver, crystal, and delicious food—but most of all we try to make them feel as much at home as we are," Carol explains.

And today, both Rucks *are* very much at home. With the remodeling and melding of furnishings complete, the couple revel in their enlarged, beautifully embellished surroundings. Says Carol: "The schoolhouse is no longer the house of my dreams. It's the home of our dreams." □

A Southern LEGACY

**Memphis designer Steve Bengel's easy
style stems from his love for old furniture,
timeworn fabrics, and his family heirlooms.**

BY MIKE BUTLER

PHOTOGRAPHY BY WILLIAM HOPKINS • PRODUCED BY MARY ANNE THOMSON
INTERIOR DESIGN BY STEVE BENGEL

Like many boys growing up in the '50s, Steve Bengel wanted to be a cowboy. That was before he fully understood the "legacy thing." Under the code of the Bengel legacy, sons and daughters are expected to inherit and cherish their share of a rich collection of antique furniture, handmade quilts, and other family heirlooms. Cowboys, on the other hand, roamed around, drank water out of creeks, and slept under the stars. Just where was Steve the cowboy going to put all that stuff when the time came?

"To my knowledge, I'm the fifth generation to hate the damned things," he says. "The legacy thing is big in my family. I don't know if it's a blessing or a curse."

In the beginning, it was probably a little of both. The past's pull on Steve was at its greatest during family visits to Cotton Plant, Arkansas, across the Mississippi River from Memphis. At his great-uncle Shelby's house, he came to know the people behind the legacy. Steve could feel the presence of his great-grandfather when he held up the old store sign from the

*Steve purchased the 1920s damask fabric for the living room draperies, **left**,
at a flea market in New York City. On the end table, an old golf trophy and a
silver hunting trophy, converted to a begonia planter, hold court
with pictures of his mother and other family photographs.*

haberdashery "W.S. Crafford & Sons," or ran his hands across the nubby wool sample quilts. "We'd have show-and-tell and log a lot of hours there," Steve recalls. "Shelby was the keeper of the keys, the custodian of the past."

Next door at Grandma's house, Steve always marveled at the clutter of Victorian and primitive furnishings. Quilts and linens everywhere reminded him of the magic that generations of women in the family had created with needle and thread.

've never really decorated for myself personally. It's what I like . . . what I'm comfortable with.

—— STEVE BENGEL

"They would collect and hoard all this ruined finery," Steve says. "They had this theory: She who dies with the most fabric wins. I always said we had more linens than money."

Steve bought into it himself, though, acquiring his first antique—a small, burled-walnut box—at age 12. And when the time came for him to head off for the University of Alabama, eager to study the liberal arts, his great-grandfather's store sign went with him.

English china graces the 1840 oak cupboard and chestnut table, left, *that Steve inherited from his great-grandmother. "Dining rooms ought to be places you can sit and be comfortable for a long time," Steve says. The timeworn fabrics* **below** *honor the past as much as the early 19th-century Pembroke table and Scottish tall clock. Liza Bones is Steve's beloved chocolate Labrador.*

Piled with books most of the time, a large Regency table in the living room also comes in handy when Steve entertains. Steve's love for family needlepoint and old fabrics can be seen in the pillows on the Hepplewhite sofa.

Steve had also discovered an affinity for interior design by then after helping his father restore and furnish a house in Cotton Plant.

Today, he relies on a highly refined design sense, an ingrained love of old things, and more than a little of the psychology he took in school to help himself and his clients make sense of their legacies.

"I think that's why every job looks different. People are all so different," Steve says. "I try to get beyond the acceptable or whatever the rage is and interpret who they are, what they're about."

During one recent project, for instance, he begged a well-to-do Memphis couple not to change a 50-year-old slipcover on a chair, which had belonged to the husband's uncle, even though they could have bought 10 chairs like it and covered them with $200-a-yard fabric.

"That would have been like putting the Mona Lisa in a chrome frame," he says. "In my family, it wasn't a point of embarrassment if you had a chair that was worn out and the fabric was bad news. It was a source of pride—the way Mama had it—and you relished that and kept it."

When Steve moved into his own Memphis apartment five years ago after a divorce, he had

*An old drawing, **opposite,** executed for the design of a needlepoint Oriental rug, is one of Steve's favorite artworks. The walking canes, riding boots, and neckties were handed down by his great-grandfather and great-uncle Shelby.*

*In the hallway **above,** cowboy boots hold a place of honor atop an American blanket chest, still bearing its original blue paint from the early 1800s. Lamps in the apartment are made from found things: old vases, biscuit tins, candlesticks, or the 70-year-old brass urn on the living room table at **left.** "I feel kind of good about recycling things," Steve says. "You're taking something else and giving it a different form and a new life."*

accumulated so much family baggage that his place could have easily become a museum. He made it his own by mixing in antiques and old fabrics he's picked up in England and on other travels. "I didn't set out to do a particular style," he says. "I've never really decorated for myself personally. It's what I like . . . what I'm comfortable with. I didn't want to preserve the past so much as the feelings of familiarity. It's nice to have a legacy. It's nice to see where you've been. It gives you a sense of identity, which I think is really important, but you cannot live in the past."

Now that he's honored the code of the Bengel legacy, Steve is rekindling the romance with his other boyhood love. Every year, he goes to Montana's Big Sky country for a cattle drive. It may not resemble the long, hard rides of old, but it's no dude outfit, either. For two weeks, anyway, a cowboy can still roam around, drink water out of creeks, and sleep under the stars. □

I guess my taste has developed to a point where I just can't get excited about something that's new.

—— STEVE BENGEL

In the guest bedroom, **left,** *linens from the family cover an old pencil-post bed made of walnut. The hatboxes and top hat belonged to Steve's great-grandfather. "He wore the brim off from tipping his hat to ladies," Steve says. A pine linen press from the mid-1800s,* **above,** *stores clothing in the master bedroom and some of Steve's favorite antique books.*

August

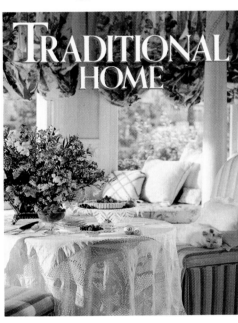

TRADITIONAL
HOME

Delightfully dressed
in seaside colors,
the Victorian
summer home of
Andrea and
Stuart Roffman is
a decorative breath
of fresh air.

Style by the SEA

By Pamela J. Wilson

PRODUCED BY ESTELLE BOND GURALNICK

*Abandoned after its original owner died in 1940, Barcliff, **above**, stared sadly out to sea for 45 years until the Roffmans, **right,** in their beach buggy, came to the rescue.*

Even on an overcast day, the entry hall entices. Floors, pickled white, and walls, glazed in periwinkle blue, play up the beauty of the white-painted woodwork and set a summery tone for the rest of the house. Floral motifs, all hand-painted, add to the room's engaging personality.

❖ ❖ ❖

The "Grey Ghost" has a new life, says Andrea Roffman, referring to the rambling Cape Cod Victorian house that she and her husband, Stuart, bought five years ago and completely renovated and revitalized inside and out.

Perched on a 60-foot cliff overlooking the Atlantic Ocean, the house's official name is Barcliff. But to the townspeople of Chatham, Massachusetts, it had long been known as the Grey Ghost—partly because of its weathered shingles, but more likely because it had been abandoned for many years.

Built as a hunting lodge at the turn of the century, Barcliff was a summer home to a New England family named

❖ ❖ ❖

On the porch below, a lattice panel, complete with a "porthole," adds architectural interest while framing a view of the pool and the fog-shrouded ocean beyond.

Style by the **SEA**

Original to the house and fully restored, the mirrored sideboard above houses Stuart and Andrea's growing collection of Bavarian china and Wedgwood oyster plates.

❖ ❖ ❖

Paine. "It was their sport to shoot game birds from the cliff," reports Andrea. After the owner's death in 1940, the house was never lived in again—at least not officially—until the Roffmans came along in the mid-1980s. So derelict was the structure when they bought it that local residents assumed that the Roffmans' plan was to tear it down and rebuild from scratch.

Actually, Stuart, a Boston real estate developer, had another motive for buying. "His plan was to restore the house for resale," says Andrea, who quickly talked him out of that. "I fell in love with the place. Even in its crumbling, depressed condition it had a certain dignity and sense of grace."

Before renovation work could begin, the Roffmans had to call in the haulers—and the exterminators. For years, local teenagers had used the house as their hangout. According to Andrea, there were 30 mattresses on the floors scattered throughout. Bathrooms contained rows of shower stalls, as in a

Style by the SEA

*As fresh as a fine summer day, the dining room can be
dressed up or down for any occasion. After a day at the beach,
the Roffmans love to gather here, whether to dine or just
sit by the window and gaze at the sea. The floor—painted a pale,
watery green—pays no mind to sand or bare feet.*

◆ ◆ ◆

Though furnished with traditional pieces, the living room is naturally suited for a relaxed way of life. English-style club chairs welcome all comers, as does the cushy settee. The floor covering is inexpensive sisal matting, prettied up with a hand-painted crisscross leaf motif. The blue and white cabana stripes on the walls look like wallpaper, but are actually painted.

◆ ◆ ◆

Well endowed with the plumpest of pillows and an assortment of antique linens, the bed **above** *combines elegance with a promise of comfort and ease.*

◆ ◆ ◆

Style by the SEA

summer camp, and there was debris everywhere. There were no light fixtures, and no kitchen—just a coal stove unchanged since the turn of the century. Moreover, there were raccoons—lots of them—freely roaming the house.

Outside, the scene was equally unsavory. Time, and fierce Atlantic storms, had taken their toll on the structure. Long gone were the front stairs, the porch railing, and numerous shingles. There was no grass, just a jungle of weeds and bushes run amok. When a workman asked if he should save the apple tree, Andrea replied,

"What apple tree?" It was so hidden in the tangle of brush, she didn't even know there was one. Not only did the Roffmans preserve the tree, they later named their daughter, Caroline, now 2, under its boughs.

The beautification of Barcliff began in the summer of 1985. Recalls Andrea: "The local residents of Chatham watched in disbelief, but with great approval, as the work progressed. . . . I'm sure they were particularly intrigued as to what we were planning to do with thirteen cubicle-size bedrooms."

What the Roffmans did do, in fact, was completely gut the top two floors of

*W*hat used to be several rooms is now a spacious, casually appointed master suite, above. Walls are festooned with hand-painted flowers and the floor is painted and pickled. Rag rugs befit the beachside setting, as do the breezy colors. A hidden asset: Curtains can be opened by the flick of a switch, allowing the Roffmans to watch the sunrise without stirring from bed.

◆ ◆ ◆

*S*urrounded by bubbles and billowy clouds overhead, Andrea, below, enjoys the tub room, a former porch now enclosed.

This delightful second-floor bathroom connects to daughter Caroline's room and a guest room. Airily adorned with crisp seersucker curtains, white floor and wall tiles, violet-strewn wallpaper, and a wonderfully whimsical swan table, the room is every inch a charmer.

◆ ◆ ◆

the house, trading the baker's dozen bedrooms for fewer, yet infinitely more spacious, sleep retreats.

Downstairs the cure wasn't quite so drastic. To be sure, a new kitchen was added and several walls were removed, but for the most part, the focus was on preserving, restoring, and embellishing the many lovely architectural details.

While restoration work was going on, Andrea called upon friend and interior designer Lynda Agger Levy to help with decorating. Says Levy: "We knew immediately that we wanted the house to have a feeling of water and sky, so the color scheme was easy—soft water tones, lots of florals, blue for the sky, green for the garden, and all the pinks and peaches that Andrea likes."

In addition to Levy, there were others in on the act. Four highly talented decorative painters—Emilie Henry, Pat Pearson and her partner Mary Woolsey, and Don Olson—contributed greatly to Barcliff's beautification. Henry, whose specialty is finding and embellishing old pieces of furniture, left her imprint in

nearly every room in the house. She also made all of the lamps. Pearson and Woolsey were responsible for many of the delightful wall motifs, including the roping with blossoms in the entryway, and the painted latticework and flowers in the master suite. Olson applied his painterly magic to the dining room floor, the blue-and-white striped living room walls, and various pieces of furniture.

All told, it took six months, and a cadre of professionals, to bring Barcliff—structurally and decoratively—back to life. Today, the former Grey Ghost, far from looking pallid, is awash with color and the kind of sparkling sunlight found only near the sea. "It has an aura," says Andrea of the rejuvenated summer house. "Whenever we're in Boston, it keeps calling us back," she adds.

So strong is Barcliff's beckoning call that the Roffmans are giving serious thought to making this their permanent, year-round home. As the old saying goes, they can't give up the ghost. □

A pair of antique beds, embellished by decorative painter Emilie Henry, is the star attraction in Caroline's room, **above.** *Henry also hand-painted the old nightstand and the faux ribbons from which a grouping of Victorian ribbon paintings seems to hang. Here, ponytailed Caroline plays with a friend and favorite baby-sitter.*

✦ ✦ ✦

Style by the **S E A**

DOWN·HOME SOPHISTICATION

*The Ganaway family, of Collierville, Tennessee,
created an elegant homestead filled with books, music, and
antiques in a restful, countrylike setting.*

BY DAN WEEKS

PHOTOGRAPHY BY RICK TAYLOR • PRODUCED BY MARY ANNE THOMSON

INTERIOR DESIGN BY STEPHEN BENGEL

The welcoming gate, ancient oaks, and Southern-farmhouse facade, *left, belie this home's in-town location and elegant informality.* Below, *Jim and Cass relax in front of their garden on a bench inherited from Cass' grandmother. "I remember it on her front porch," says Cass.*

What attracted Jim and Cass Ganaway to their Tennessee home was space. That's understandable: They have five children. But the kind of space they really wanted had to do with the *quality* of their environment. When you walk through the gate of "Ancient Oaks," named for the towering trees in the home's front yard, you enter one family's personal domain.

"Our home is real important to us," says Cass with the gentle inflections of her native Mississippi. "I feel like everyone needs stability, roots, and tradition—a place that's peaceful and positive. We even enjoy spending vacation time here."

Inside, that sense of peace and continuity is provided by a houseful of Southern antiques, books, musical instruments, and Cass' handwork. Outside, there's a garden, animals for the children to care for and play with, and the landscaping projects that Jim works on for relaxation.

"Our first home was a brand-new house in a Houston subdivision," says Cass. "Right away, we didn't feel comfortable living there. Here, we can live the way we want to." It's that kind of independent spirit—plus a reverence for the past and a sophisticated eye—that has created the Ganaways' adopted homestead.

A Renaissance Revival hall tree, right, *displays Cass' collection of hats, and provides a place for umbrellas and scarves. The front door and sidelights are original; the wainscoting was added from another early Southern home.*

Our home is real important to us. I feel like everyone needs stability, roots, and tradition—a place that's peaceful and positive. We even enjoy spending vacation time here.

—— CASS GANAWAY

A punch bowl with a grape-and-Bacchus design and pearl-handled silverware add elegance to Cass' table of desserts, right. *Brown walls provide a soft background for a collection of Staffordshire plates,* above. *In keeping with the house's age, the table, carpet, and chairs date from about 1850.*

"My folks got us into collecting antiques before we got out of college," says Jim. "They collected American country, so that's where we started." The Ganaways then became interested in Empire ("a nice transition between country and Victorian") and sophisticated country pieces. They eventually narrowed their focus to Southern antiques, especially those from Tennessee and Mississippi, where Cass and Jim grew up. "I think Southern pieces fit the house better," Jim says.

"Our interest is in history," explains Cass, who is documenting the origins of the pieces they own. "For us, owning a piece of antique furniture is another way to learn how people used to live. Each

An antique brass student lamp, bone and horn corkscrews, and platters from Cass' collection top a drop-front desk in a dining room corner, left. *The ironstone pitcher and bowl are part of a larger collection kept in the kitchen.*

one is a history lesson. I know that they're ours for just a little while, and then we'll pass them on to our children, who will reassimilate them into another home, another collection. So far, they all enjoy the antiques, and that pleases me."

As for her own home, "We wanted a feeling of relaxed formality," says Cass. "There is not a room in the house that has matched furniture. But to me, the mixture of styles and colors makes the house feel more personal. Nothing is perfect; it's all accessible, touchable."

Part of that "touchability" results from the fact that the house reflects the Ganaways' interests and talents. Cass sews, and has done some of the window treatments and many of the pieces of needlework seen around the house. "I don't want to wait till the children are grown to make them their own Christmas stockings and special things," she says.

Cass also cans, pickles, and tends to the herb and flower gardens, sometimes turning up Civil War-era relics in the soil after a rain. Jim enjoys working outside the house, and their older children also collect things—such as toy soldiers and celluloid toy figures from the '40s—which can be found decorating their rooms.

Finally, the whole family shares an interest in making music and in reading. "I keep children's books all over the house," says Cass. "Whenever somebody wants to read a book, we can sit down and do it right there. It's part of our daily ritual."

"To me, the living room is a music room," says Cass. "It offers us a place to sit and enjoy company, music, or a book." The needlepoint sampler, English tea set, and American Empire mahogany chairs, left, all date from the mid 1800s. The Empire mahogany table and chairs, above, are backed by Cass' growing collection of antique books.

The sitting room left *is a favorite place for family gatherings. An American Gothic Revival chair, an electrified* Gone With the Wind *lamp, and an old cabbage-rose chintz coverlet on the love seat add to the room's charm.*

Half piano, half organ, the melodian above *is part of the Ganaways' collection of antique instruments, as are the child's violin and unidentified mandolinlike piece.*

Jim built the circular patio below *from Arkansas fieldstone. It takes advantage of fragrant hostas and garden views.*

*F*or me, it's all about my children. Whether I'm reading a story, arranging flowers, or baking a pound cake, I do it because I feel it will add to their memories and experiences.

—— CASS GANAWAY

Another ritual, during the growing season, is gardening. Jim tends to the vegetables; Cass grows flowers and culinary herbs— "plants that either attract wildlife close to the house, or things that can be dried or are edible," she says. "I plant mostly native varieties, so they're very easy to grow. I take into account how the house is situated, how the light comes through the trees. It takes a long time to see what is called for, to know what to add where. Everything we've done," she says, surveying the house and the grounds, "has really evolved as we saw what was needed." □

 *On the back porch,* above, *an American farm table holds vegetables, handmade slate trivets, and oil lamps; graniteware adorns the wall.*

October

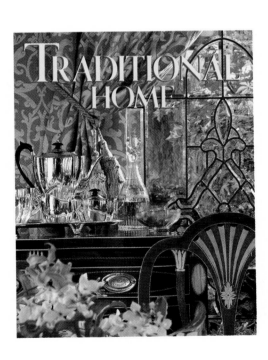

Getting
Comfortable

BY HEATHER J. WRIGHT

*Comfort gets top billing
in designer Lynda Levy's
suburban Boston home.*

PHOTOGRAPHY BY D. RANDOLPH FOULDS
PRODUCED BY ESTELLE BOND GURALNICK
INTERIOR DESIGN BY LYNDA LEVY

s a hard-working interior designer, Lynda Levy's days are busy and full of stimulation. When she comes home, however, things are different. "I really look forward to coming home to calmness," Lynda says. "That's why comfort, quiet, and relaxation were my first considerations when designing my own home."

The 60-year-old colonial home Lynda shares with her lawer husband, Franklin, and son, Justin, is just outside Boston in Newton, Massachusetts. When the Levys first saw the house, the exterior was painted bright red (Lynda likes only white houses), and the inside was dark and gloomy. Nevertheless, Lynda knew she wanted it. She could see the possibilities: The rounded brick patio in the front had charm, the house could be painted white, a fragrant all-white garden could be planted, and Sunday brunches could be hosted there in springtime.

Also to Linda's delight, the rooms inside the house were unusually large even though the ceilings were just 7½ feet tall. "The master bedroom is as large as the living room," Lynda says, with glee. "That's very unusual for a house of this age."

It has been six years now since the Levys moved in, and there has been continual improvement. Even

The library, **left,** *features cheerful, floral chintz. The draperies and the artistic curtain rod were part of a showhouse room Lynda created. After the show, she redesigned them for her own home.*

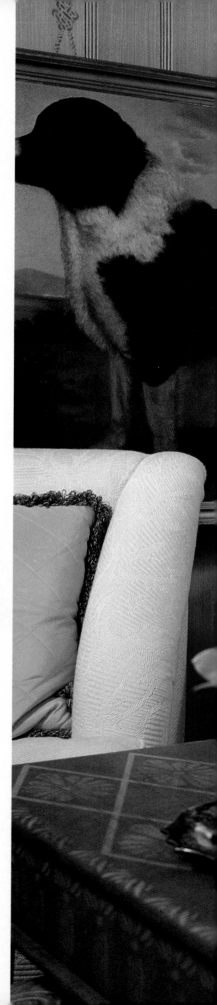

Getting Comfortable

The antique oil painting of a St. Bernard hanging in the library, right, lends a touch of whimsy to the room's cozy mood. Justin Levy's self-portraits, created when he was in first and second grades, are showcased on the windowsill. A new decoupaged lamp and custom pillows contribute to the rich raspberry color scheme.

so, Lynda believes her first projects made the biggest difference in how she ultimately feels about her home. She removed dark green carpet, uncovering wood floors, which she then painted. She took down heavy draperies and gave pea green walls new life with fresh coats of cream, taupe, and warm raspberry paint. The interiors are now a comfortable blend of soft colors, elegant patterns, and varied textures.

Though most of the house reflects Lynda's preference for a more subdued look, the library, shown on *pages 122–123* and *right,* showcases vibrant patterns of floral and paisley in shades of red and pink. "This is where Justin feels most comfortable," says

I really look forward to coming home to calmness. That's why comfort, quiet, and relaxation were my first considerations when designing my own home.

—— LYNDA LEVY

Franklin (called Biff), Lynda, and son Justin, above, relax on their front steps. Lynda designed the ornamental railing that encloses the front flower garden.

When the Levys found their colonial house, left, it was painted bright red. Lynda hated the color, but Justin loved it. "Whenever I drove in, I didn't feel at home," Lynda says. "I finally got my way and painted it white."

*Lynda calls the living room, **left**, her **belle epoque** room. "It's a little more formal than the rest of the house," she explains. Silk, taffeta draperies, and an antique linen tablecloth lend quiet elegance.*

*Because the taupe and soft blue living room is almost monochromatic, the artwork in it really stands out. **Below**, an oil reproduction of a Degas ballet scene, originally done in chalk, gives the room a burst of color and romance.*

Getting Comfortable

Lynda. "And anyway, I like to have one room that's alive with color. A home tends to float if *everything* is light."

As an interior designer, Lynda participates in many show-houses, and the Levy house is sprinkled with many pieces from those shows. "You can incorporate a lot of oddities in a home if you're smart about it," Lynda says. "I really enjoy taking furniture out of one situation and playing with it so that it fits comfortably into even some unlikely places," she says.

That practical spirit is at play throughout the house. For the library, for instance, Lynda skillfully pared down a bank of draperies from a showhouse into a shorter window treatment. She used the painted curtain rod they were hung on, and she salvaged extra fabric to cover the sofa and wingback chair.

In the Levys' spacious bedroom, the look is restrained but sumptuous. The chair below, upholstered in an Aubusson carpet-pattern, dates to the 1890s. The antique, shell-motif cupboard in the corner showcases Lynda's majolica collection and a few of her celluloid clocks.

☙ *Lynda uses her painted peach-on-peach bedroom mantel,* **above,** *to display her celluloid treasures. She's been an avid collector for 18 years.*

☙ *The master bedroom,* **below,** *is touched with witty details, including a wonderful painted faux headboard. "I've never had time to look for a headboard!" Lynda says. "That's the story of my life."*

I enjoy taking furniture out of one situation and playing with it so that it fits comfortably into even some unlikely places.

—— LYNDA LEVY

Getting Comfortable

In the living room *(pages 126-127)*, where the quiet palette is taupe with delicate touches of blue, a circa-1900 oil painting of a young girl by Alexander Stoddard Kent was the inspiration for the color and mood. Lynda laughs when she recalls: "I tried to get several of my clients to buy that wonderful painting. When they didn't want it, I realized it was fate. I loved the painting myself and used it."

A taupe and cream color scheme also is tastefully echoed throughout this house, but no more beautifully than in the dining room *(pages 130-131)*. There, the palette is translated via nubby cotton upholstered chairs, plaid silk drapery, and linen-covered walls and moldings. "It's the simplest room in the house and also my favorite," Lynda says. Because it is a small room, Lynda has two tables instead of one large one. "I do wish the room were a bit bigger, but since it isn't, this solution works well." One table, a plywood round, is charmingly disguised with overcloths for everyday use and intimate

The console table at right opens out to seat 14, but in everyday life doubles as a pretty pedestal for a collection of antique decoupaged boxes. The breakfast room bar, below, is delicately and whimsically painted to look as if botanical prints are tacked up.

Getting Comfortable

parties. The other, a console table, doubles as a sideboard when not opened out to seat up to 14 for large dinners. To make the room feel as spacious as possible, Lynda raised the curtain valances to the ceiling.

Three years ago when they remodeled their 1950s-style kitchen, the Levys built a breakfast room with the tall ceiling they wish they had throughout the house. Lynda takes full advantage of the height by furnishing the room with overscaled chairs and a formidable whitewashed armoire that houses the television and stereo equipment. The room is airy and light with an oak floor stylishly painted with diamonds—some rubbed, others sponged for texture. Shirred valances with a lovely grape and leaf motif leave the windows mostly bare to let the sun stream in.

The remodeled kitchen is just a few steps above the breakfast

The dining room, below, is redolent with simple elegance. The taupe and cream theme is layered with gold-framed botanicals, an antique chandelier, and cherished Matisse prints that the Levys received as a wedding gift.

*"I love having
a fireplace in the
breakfast room,"*
says Lynda. This ingeniously
decorated mantel is one of Lynda's
showhouse relics. Once stained
mahogany, it was cut down and
painted so it appears to be faced with
leaf-embossed tiles.

room and shares its airy mood. Pine cabinets, glazed in cream and taupe, look like handsome furniture. The central island Lynda designed is pretty *and* functional— it's a worktop that converts to a table for seven. "The kitchen is the most important room for a family. You end up spending a lot of quality time there if it feels right," Lynda says. "It's the best room to renovate if you're only able to do one."

Lynda admits that her own busy schedule means she is taking one room at a time at home. And she *does* have a few rooms left. Her current project is Biff's upstairs study. "He's working on a mystery novel," says Lynda. "You'll never guess where it takes place . . . in a designers' showhouse." □

Getting Comfortable

🌿 *Various shades of green were used as accent colors in the breakfast room,* **above.** *To further bring the beauty of the outside in, Lynda put valances on windows instead of full curtains. The round table is new, but the chairs surrounding it were retrieved from yet another showhouse.*

🌿 *Lynda designed the new kitchen,* **below,** *to replace the awkward '50s-style design they inherited. The large center island functions as a worktop and snack bar, and has lots of storage. The pine stove hood conceals an exhaust system and is painted with an allover leaf motif and a small pear.*

PARTNERS IN STYLE

BY PAMELA J. WILSON

PHOTOGRAPHY BY JON JENSEN
PRODUCED BY BONNIE MAHARAM

Assuredly furnished with a pleasing mix of traditional, contemporary, and country elements, the Long Island home of Barbara and Michael Orenstein is a fine example of fresh thinking and personal style.

The Orensteins, above, on their sun porch, have done everything possible to capitalize on the natural beauty that surrounds the house. Wherever possible, windows have been left completely uncovered, or, as in the living room, left, treated simply with barely there panels of light-filtering lace.

Bathed in dappled sunlight, the white brick, 1920s-vintage house, right, was a favorite of Barbara and Michael long before they bought it.

◆ ◆ ◆

As the English essayist and critic John Ruskin once said, "When love and skill work together, expect a masterpiece."

Surely this holds true for Barbara and Michael Orenstein. Partners in marriage for 24 years, and—of late—partners in Barbara's 10-year-old interior design business, they can both take a bow for the successful renovation and decorative redo of their lovely Long Island home.

When the house came on the market in 1984, the couple was quick to pounce. The Orensteins both grew up in Hewlett Bay Park, and unbeknownst to each other, had always considered this their favorite house in the area. However, it wasn't until they saw the "For Sale" sign that they discovered their mutual attraction for the manorly 1920s-era dwelling.

In the living and dining rooms, dark-age color schemes have been banished. Walls, once a dispirited shade of blue, are now the brightest of uplifting white.

Richly textured with English antiques, a marvelous green-painted sideboard, a new Oriental rug, and an unusual hexagonal, white tile floor, the dining room, opposite *and* right, *is further enhanced by the presence of white and a flooding of natural, ambient light. Fresh flowers—peonies on the sideboard and blue cornflowers in individual bud vases—are fetching accompaniments to the scene.*

Upon entering the foyer, below, *guests are given the red carpet treatment—but in this case, the carpet is an antique Boukara rug.*

◆ ◆ ◆

"We were out for a drive, and we both shrieked in unison when we saw the sign," she recalls.

Had it not been for their long-held attraction for the house—an L-shaped structure with weathered, white-painted brick—the Orensteins might well have kept driving. The grounds and gardens, once beautifully and meticulously maintained, had been sadly neglected.

So, too, the interior spaces. The plaster was crumbling, the ceilings leaked badly, and the wood floors had seen better days. Cosmetically, the house had been completely ignored for at least 30 years and, as a result, lacked a sense of identity. Quips Barbara, "If houses could talk, this one would have said 'Who am I?'"

But never mind. The Orensteins, undeterred by the drawbacks, opted for ownership. "You just don't find many houses like this today," says Barbara, referring to numerous architectural details that make the house special. "We were enamored with the moldings, the paneling, the Dutch doors, the built-ins, and all of the little nooks and niches. There's even a tiny room designed especially to hold a telephone and a chair."

The Orensteins traded three small rooms to make way for a singularly spectacular kitchen. Fitted with top-of-the-line appliances and all manner of amenities, the room, according to Barbara, is the heartbeat of the house. Mellow stained-oak floors and white-painted paneled walls are country-style counterpoints for the up-to-the-minute setting.

◆ ◆ ◆

In refurbishing the house, the pair's approach was to preserve the architectural character, but not pay homage to it. "It was never our intention to create a period look. We love antiques and all things English, but at the same time, we're not slaves to the past or to convention," Barbara says.

The revitalized decorating scheme is a happy meeting ground of time-honored and up-to-the-minute ideas. In the main living areas, antiques co-star with contemporary and country pieces—to the beautiful benefit of all. Glass-top tables, far from looking like untraditional interlopers, are energizing adjuncts for the venerable antiques.

Accessories, like the furnishings, are an admix. Objects of the Orensteins' affections range from old bird cages, antique quill boxes, and books to collections of antique majolica, candlesticks, and numerous needlepoint pillows, mostly new. "We always advise our clients to build on collections, be they fine antiques, heirlooms, or just-for-fun finds," Barbara says, adding, "Without a doubt, they're the best ingredients for giving a house essential character and personality."

In the living room and dining room, dark-age color schemes have been banished. Walls, once a dispirited shade of blue, are now the brightest of

When it comes to casual dining, the Orensteins have several inviting options. For lunch and light suppers, the kitchen eating area, right, gets preference.

At breakfast time, the former butler's pantry, above, beckons. Referred to now as the Tutor Room, it's where the couple's daughters met with their tutor when in high school.

✦ ✦ ✦

*H*ugged by green semigloss walls, the master bedroom, right, is a dreamy oasis, designed for respite and repose. Refined appointments include the brass and black iron bed from England, luxurious linens, and a lovely antique wedding-pattern quilt. At the opposite end of the room, below, white-painted cabinetry keeps the green scheme from overpowering. Here, a fanciful Victorian wicker chair is teamed with a marble-topped English pine desk.

*I*n the guest bath, left, the Orensteins played favorites with a French-style sink, a seldom-met mirrored towel bar, and a tiny window trimmed with lace.

◆ ◆ ◆

uplifting white. Though not usually associated with traditional schemes, white, according to the Orensteins, can do much to divest a room of dated and dowdy notions. "It has wonderful restorative powers, especially in older homes," says Barbara.

Window treatments, upstairs and down, are barely there lace panels or, in some cases, not there at all. Says Barbara, "We decided to forgo heavy or elaborate draperies and curtains in favor of sunlight and bringing the beauty of the outside in."

Rightfully so. The Orensteins' newly landscaped grounds are exceptionally gaze-worthy. Where overgrowth and weeds once reigned, there are magnificent, parklike lawns dotted with stately trees, formal boxwoods, rhododendrons, and colorful English-style perennial gardens. Crushed gravel paths invite leisurely strolling, and there are iron benches, strategically placed, for those who prefer to contemplate the scenery while sitting.

When not tending to the revitalization of their own house, the Orensteins keep very busy seeing to the beautification of others'. It has been nearly three years since Michael sold his curtain and drapery manufacturing business in order to link up, business-wise, with Barbara.

"It seemed like the natural thing to do," she says, adding, "Michael has a wonderful textile background, and we've always had an uncanny meeting of minds when it comes to interior design. We can go into the same store, separately, at different times of day, then later discover that we loved or hated exactly the same things."

Now that the Orensteins' daughters, Elizabeth and Heather, are off at college, it is just the two of them—at home *and* at work. And whereas some people might find this too much togetherness, the couple are content. "We can't complain," states Barbara. "For both of us, it's like working with our best friend." □

BY PAMELA J. WILSON

PHOTOGRAPHY BY GENE JOHNSON
PRODUCED BY NANCY E. INGRAM
INTERIOR DESIGN BY S.R. HUGHES & DAUGHTERS
LANDSCAPE DESIGN BY JACK CRAIN

Lakeside Allure

Nestled on the shores of an idyllic, 23-acre lake, Linda's stacked-stone ranch house, *opposite,* is a wonderfully secluded retreat. On mornings when Linda, *left,* takes a prebreakfast canoe ride, Bruno, the neighbor's dog and Linda's walking companion, is there to see her off.

The living room, *below,* with its panoramic window wall, offers a fabulous front row seat for watching nature's ever-changing theater.

T hough only minutes away from downtown Oklahoma City, Linda Lambert's lakeside home is light-years away from the madding crowd.

I can't believe I was lucky enough to find this place.
It's a sanctuary where I can retreat from pressure and spend
time alone enjoying my home and nature.

T hough she's by no means a recluse, business executive Linda Lambert dearly loves her privacy. As a partner in her family-owned business in Oklahoma City, her workaday life is always fast-paced, and often hectic.

After work and on weekends, what Linda seeks is solitude—the blissful, laid-back variety. And she has it. Her lakeside house is an idyllic hideaway, worlds removed from the daily grind, though it's just a short commute to her office.

Linda purchased the house in 1990, shortly after moving from Tulsa to Oklahoma City. What attracted her initially was not so much the house itself—a rather modest 1940s stacked-stone ranch—but the heavenly setting. Along with a 23-acre lake that rivals Golden Pond (of movie fame) for serene beauty, there are hundreds of trees—oaks, dogwoods, and redbuds—that encircle the house, and the lake, like a leafy necklace.

To say the least, Linda loves it here. "I can't believe I was lucky enough to find this place," she says. "It's a sanctuary where I can retreat from pressure and spend time alone enjoying my home and nature."

The interior of the house features an airy, open floor plan, beautifully suited for the setting. Vaulted pecky cypress ceilings and flagstone floors are natural assets, as are the magnificent floor-to-ceiling windows

W ith help from her interior designers, Linda fashioned the living room and dining nook, *left,* exactly to her liking. Many furnishings, including the ultra-comfortable reading chair by the window and the pair of chenille-covered club chairs, once belonged to her parents. Only the fabrics are new.

L olling by the lakeside is one of Linda's favorite pastimes. In late spring and summer, this hammock, *right,* becomes her third bedroom.

Embraced by newly built bookshelves, the dining alcove, *right,* is an intimate room within a room. Charming accoutrements include a reproduction English gateleg table paired with a love seat and a trio of heirloom chairs. Swing-arm lamps, with fanciful fringed shades, shed light on the scene.

Refreshed with paint and glass-fronted cupboard doors, the once-dated kitchen, *left,* looks new again.

I told them I wanted a home that was informal, cozy, plump, and not too serious.

—— LINDA LAMBERT

that face the scenic lake. "I knew instantly that Mother Nature had to be the star of this house," Linda says, adding, "I wanted to bring the outside in so it would be hard to distinguish between the living areas and the world of nature outside."

Linda's mandate to her interior designers, Sara and Sallie Hughes and Beth Sachse of S.R. Hughes & Daughters, was simple. "I told them I wanted a home that was informal, cozy, plump, and not too serious," she says. When asked to define "plump," Linda answered with a smile: "It's an overstuffed chair I can sink into at night and never be found again."

Heeding the mandate, the designers filled the living room with a variety of overstuffed, pleasantly plump, seating pieces. Linda's favorite "sink-into-it"

spot is a cushy chair strategically placed in front of the panoramic living room window (see *pages 147 and 149*). The chair, newly re-covered in a whimsical Oriental print, was originally her father's favorite reading chair.

It took some prodding—on the part of the designers—to convince Linda to incorporate other recently acquired family heirlooms into the decor. She was particulary averse to using a gold-toned Oriental rug, fearing it looked dated and too formal. "That rug had been in my parents' home when I was growing up, and I thought it looked wonderful there, but here it reminded me of the 1950s," she relates. But the designers persisted. "They convinced me that this rug was perfect for the neutral color scheme I wanted and now, I have to agree, it is," she says.

In keeping with the "not too serious" part of the mandate, the designers and

Linda decided to have fun with a set of formal dining chairs, also old family pieces. The cushions, once covered in silk, now sport a fetching, country-style check fabric. And each pair of cushions has been treated differently—one pair has pleats, another has scallops, and two others have gathers. All are delightful and perfectly suited to the casual appeal of the house.

As much as she loves her refurbished surroundings, Linda prefers to be outdoors. "I'm outside all the time now. I take a walk around the lake every afternoon after work. I read the Sunday *New York Times* out on the boat dock. In the late spring and summer, the hammock becomes my third bedroom," she says.

But more than just laze by the lake, Linda is actively involved in the care and upkeep of the secluded, tree-studded grounds. "This house needed someone to give nature top priority, and I'm willing to make that commitment in return for privacy and serenity," she says. To this end, she hired landscape designer Jack Crain to create a plan for preserving and enhancing the grounds. She is also collaborating with an urban forester to replant trees in such a way that when one dies, a new one is ready to take its place. Recently, rather than cut down a dead tree entirely, she had the trunk sculpted into a giant rabbit, who now presides like a friendly sentinel over the grounds.

For all its seclusion, Linda's retreat is easy to find. "Look for the mailbox with the pansies growing out of the top," she says with a laugh. "You can't miss it. It's my signature—and besides, who else do you know who waters their mailbox?" □

The master bath, *left,* with its whirlpool tub and view of the lake, provides a perfect place for sybaritic pursuits. Here, Linda used yet another heirloom—her father's bookshelves—to display mementos and photos of her family and friends.

Even the master bedroom, *above,* is closely connected to nature. On warm nights, with the windows open, Linda is lulled to sleep by the sound of water lapping gently on the shore. In the morning, she is awakened by a chorus of chirping birds.

December

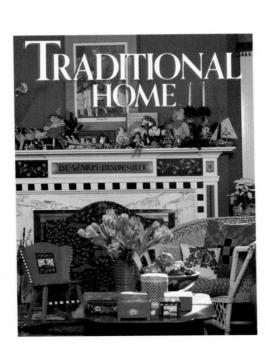

Christmas *at* Captain's Farm

BY PAMELA J. WILSON
PRODUCED BY ESTELLE BOND GURALNICK
PHOTOGRAPHY BY D. RANDOLPH FOULDS

Gracing a snowy Connecticut landscape, Captain's Farm is the kind of place we all wish we could come home to.

Exterior photographs by Dan Smith

It begins to feel a lot like Christmas the minute Captain's Farm, **left** *and* **above,** *comes into view. But the snowy scene and the red-ribboned lanterns are only teasers for the holiday mood that imbues the house itself.*

In the living room, **opposite,** *a traditionally trimmed fir tree keeps company with an 1820s Baltimore Federal settee, topped with a rag rug.*

*The table in the reception room, **right**, usually is heaped with books and decorative objects, but here it stands ready for the party, with Christmas punch in an English porcelain bowl. **Above**, the "King of Tarts" is one of many ornaments given to the homeowner by friends.*

There are some who would say, as Robert Louis Stevenson once did, that it is better to travel hopefully than to arrive. No doubt, on occasion, this is true. But there are destinations where reality not only meets, but exceeds, all expectations.

One such place is Captain's Farm—the Connecticut country home of Manhattanite Edward Lee Cave. Here, approximately 10 days before Christmas, Cave and his partner, Dan Smith, host a Christmas house party for 18 to 24 of their friends.

"Actually," he says, "it's a practice family Christmas," adding, "Most guests spend December 25th with their own families, so the festivities here are just a warm-up."

Warm-up or not, it's a wonderful, highly anticipated event. Some of the invitees live in the tiny, rural hamlet where Captain's Farm is located, but others— including many of Cave and Smith's dearest friends— travel hundreds of miles to attend this much-loved annual gathering.

With good reason. Cave, a consummate traditionalist, goes to great lengths to see

Captain's Farm

Cave was destined to own the magnificent
1795 Philadelphia secretary that now graces the
winter garden conservatory. He had eyed it for
years—first at an antiques show in Hartford, then
at the New York Armory show, and again in an ad
in an antiques magazine—before finally
succumbing to its lure.

that his guests' wish lists are completely fulfilled.

"I still believe in Santa Claus," Cave reveals, adding, "The reason I believe is because I finally discovered his true identity—oneself." To this end, he provides for everything. First there's the setting. Were Hollywood producers to scout for a picture-perfect location to film a Christmas movie, Captain's Farm would surely be a contender. Surrounded by sheltering pine trees, glistening lanes, and gentle, snow-blanketed hills, the picturesque 1740s farm beckons like a parent with welcoming arms open wide.

❧ *Except for several new seating pieces, all furnishings in the living room,* **left** *and* **below,** *are American antiques. The table in front of the love seat is a grain-painted sewing box now used to store Christmas cards.*

Captain's Farm

Then there's the holiday ambience. Returning guests know—and first-timers sense—that they're in for a treat once they've crossed the threshold. If a house could be likened to a carol, this one would be Mel Torme's "The Christmas Song."

Awaiting are all of the accoutrements one could ever dream of—fires crackling, chestnuts roasting, champagne chilling, and tables groaning with good things to eat.

Classic decorations include handmade swags of boxwood and laurel, bowls heaped with pinecones (all gathered from the property), Della Robbia wreaths, scented candles, and a profusion of poinsettias and other flowering plants.

On tap, too, are exquisitely trimmed Christmas trees with presents for everyone piled beneath. "I love preparing and giving gifts, but must admit I'm painfully embarrassed at receiving them," Cave confesses.

Nevertheless, guests do come bearing gifts, not just for the host, but for each other. They also come bearing pets. "Oh, yes," says Cave, "it's very important to bring your pet to the party— they all get presents, too."

Miraculously, in the 10 years that Cave and Smith have been putting on the Christmas celebration, there have been no pet-related disasters. Also thus far, animal attendees have been limited to well-behaved dogs and cats.

"I have friends who've been dying to bring their 19-pound pet rabbit, but so far I haven't relented," Cave says.

Though he now lives and works in New York City, Cave was born and raised in Virginia, where he learned all there is to know about Southern hospitality. "Christmas," he says, "is a time when every dish should be overflowing."

To ensure that all dishes are just that, Cave calls upon local friends Jimmy and Barbara Cavar to cater the Christmas feast. The menu is

According to Cave, it wasn't until 1760 that American homes had dining rooms. People ate wherever it was most pleasant, a practice he endorses. The hearth, **opposite,** *is used in winter, but when spring arrives, meals are served in the conservatory.*

Windows, **above,** *are decked with pinecone swags secured with ribbons.*

Captain's Farm

162

Captain's Farm

traditional, consisting of turkey and all manner of trimmings. Also true to Southern tradition, there's a delicious Smithfield ham.

The Cavars, in addition to organizing and cooking the dinner, are guests at the party as well. "Following the meal and the exchange of gifts, Jimmy leads us all in singing favorite Christmas carols," Cave says.

Part of the pleasure of attending a country house party—be it during the Christmas season or any other time of year—is having the opportunity to relax and renew old acquaintances. Many of Cave and Smith's friends are also friends with each other, and this is the one time of year they're able to get together as a group.

In the afternoon before the party, guests find much to engage them. Raconteurs sit by the open fires, swapping stories and each other's news. Outdoor types are lured by the prospect of taking long walks on the property, and readers—should they be so inclined—can peruse the books in Cave's extensive art reference library.

When the party's over and it's time to return home, guests leave with their pets, their presents, and a year's worth of wonderful memories in tow. □

BELIEVE

a merry
❖ E N G E L B R E I T ❖
Christmas

At Christmastime, the St. Louis home of greeting card designer
Mary Engelbreit is a world of Yuletide enchantment.

By Pamela J. Wilson

PRODUCED BY MARY ANNE THOMSON WITH SUSAN DAVIDSON
PHOTOGRAPHY BY BARBARA ELLIOTT MARTIN

Mary Engelbreit. Even if the name of this talented artist doesn't jingle a bell, the odds are excellent that you've given (or been the happy recipient of) one of her highly popular greeting cards. Noted for their whimsy and warm sentimental appeal, Mary's cards speak to our hearts and unfailingly make us feel good.

The same can be said of Mary's own house—most certainly at Christmastime. Here, to the delight of her husband and business manager, Philip Delano, and their young sons, Evan, 10, and Will, 8, Mary goes all out. Stepping into her house—an inviting Dutch colonial in Webster Groves, Missouri— is like stepping into one of her fanciful greeting cards. Every room is stuffed, much like a stocking, with wonderful surprises.

❇ *With a special talent for making spirits bright, Mary, **above**, festooned her front door with purple paint and sunflowers.*

*Mary gladdened the mantel, **left**, with a gathering of cherished old toys. The rocking chair in front of the hearth was painted by Mary for son Will when he was born. Promptly dubbed "Good Will" by his grandfather, Will's nickname has stuck, even to the rocker.*

*Anything miniature is magical for Mary, and her constellation of collections is always expanding. The wee chairs on the table **above** are relics from the dollhouse her father built for her when she was a child. The lampshade, with its galaxy of heavenly red cherries, is a Mary original.*

As colorful and
effervescent as a bowl
of Christmas cheer,
Mary's living room
endears all who
enter—even bah-
humbug types.
Furnished with
collections, heirlooms,
and flea market finds,
the room is an
amalgam of Mary's
"absolutely favorite"
things. Especially
loved are the garlands
of glittering glass
beads that swag the
tree; they once
belonged to Mary's
grandmother.

ENGELBREIT

"Christmas is my favorite holiday, my favorite time of year," says Mary. In fact, she is so fond of the season that she keeps many of her holiday decorations—her ever-increasing collections of Santas and reindeer, tiny trees, old Christmas books, and fetching snowmen—on display all year long.

No one, least of all her family and friends, finds this strange. "I don't think they even notice," she relates. "The Christmas collections sort of fade into the background other times of the year. But I like to keep them out. They remind me of the innocent, joyful childhood feelings we all have at Christmas."

Joy is what Mary—her art, her house, her approach to life—is all about. A philosopher as well as an artist, her sayings range from gentle imperatives such as "Bloom where you are planted," to such skewered spoonerisms as "Life is just a chair of bowlies."

*Among Mary's myriad collections, old children's books, including these, **above**, rank among her favorites and provide a great source of inspiration for her greeting cards.*

*To climb the hand-painted stairsteps, **opposite**, is to take a sentimental journey past the most important people in the Delanos' lives—their children, their families, and dear friends. Remembrances such as these, framed and otherwise, meander happily throughout the house.*

*Traditionally, trimming the tree is Mary's preserve, but Evan and Will serve as overseers, ensuring that their favorite ornaments are hung with care in the forefront. **Above**, Philip and the boys have just given high marks to Mary's tree-decorating efforts.*

171

"I don't write all of the quotes," she says. "I find a lot of them in books, or they're things I hear—funny things the kids will say. I like quotes with a positive outlook, those that say, 'Life is going on right now, enjoy it, don't wait for it to happen.' "

At Christmastime—at all times—Mary's positive outlook is manifest. On the fancifully painted living room fireplace (see *page 166*), there's an inscription that implores us to "Be warm inside and out." And in this house, we are. Affably amassed on the mantel are a legion of lovable toys and miniatures, all waiting for Christmas Day to dawn. Elsewhere, everywhere, are happy gatherings of Mary's many collections— her "stuff," as Evan and Will refer to her treasures. "There's hardly anything I don't collect," she says, with a sheepish grin, adding, "My friends have no trouble finding gifts for me."

Assorted St. Nicks, and a tiny ornament-studded tree, above, are engaging accompaniments for the table, set with family heirlooms for Christmas Day brunch.

❀

Not to be outdone by the family's festivities, Bunny, Mr. Bear, and Dolly, above, sit at a table laid out for their own Yuletide party. Mary painted Mr. Bear's tiny chair for Evan when he was born. The tea set, with matching cloth napkins and place mats, was designed by Mary.

The dining room, right, delectably decked out for the holidays, is a pleasure to behold. Especially engaging is the hutch— filled to capacity with Mary's much-loved collection of old and new baby plates and cups. Interspersed with the dishware are candy canes and fruit.

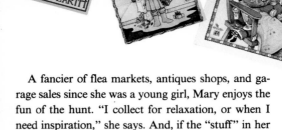

A fancier of flea markets, antiques shops, and garage sales since she was a young girl, Mary enjoys the fun of the hunt. "I collect for relaxation, or when I need inspiration," she says. And, if the "stuff" in her boys' bedrooms is any indication, she seems to have passed on her acquisitive genes to them.

Mary remembers her own childhood—her first some might say—filled with swings and sandboxes, her bare feet on cold, slippery grass, blithely chasing lightning bugs. But most of all, she remembers a childhood filled with books.

"I love books," she says, "particularly the old ones I grew up with. They're where I get most of my inspiration." Mary learned to draw by copying her mother's and her grandmother's picture books. The books' nostalgic, winsome appeal has clearly left its mark on her art.

Checkerboards and cherries are two of Mary's favorite motifs, and they pop up in pleasing ways thoughout the house. Opposite, checkered tile adds graphic charm to the family room fireplace, with its exuberant mantel and a Victorian card table cleverly used as a firescreen.

With great patience, Evan (on left) and Will, below, waited to have their picture taken before devouring the delicious props.

To this day, Mary saves—and continues to collect—old children's books. There are stacks of them, shelves crammed with them throughout the house. And they don't just sit gathering dust. She still loves to read them, and now, so do her sons.

"We have seven or eight Christmas books that are the boys' favorites, and each night leading up to Christmas, we'll read one of them. On Christmas Eve, we all gather in the living room to read *'Twas the Night Before Christmas*," Mary relates.

There are other traditions in the Delano house, all born of one word: Believe. Muses Mary, "Evan and Will changed the whole idea of Christmas for me. They made it like when I was little. They brought back all the magic of believing, and they helped me to believe again, too." □

Mary fitted the ❈ *master bath, **above**, not with an ordinary sink, but with a majestic dining room buffet, metamorphosed with white paint, marble, and new fixtures.*

As a young girl, Mary learned to draw by copying children's picture books. One book, Rimskittle, *had great impact on her drawing style. Eventually, the beloved book fell apart, but Mary salvaged some of the pages, had them framed, then hung them below the window seat, **above**.*

*Festively beribboned in red, the walnut bed, **opposite**, was crafted by Mary's great-grandfather. The chest at the foot of the bed, with its blue paint and dainty vines, was purchased—and painted—by Mary at the age of 16. It was her first such project, but certainly not her last.*

A Shopkeeper's *Holiday*

BY PAMELA J. WILSON
PHOTOGRAPHY BY GENE JOHNSON
PRODUCED BY NANCY E. INGRAM

In short order, Tracy Lorton decided to leave her job in New York, return to her hometown of Tulsa, open a shop, and buy a 1930s cottage. Now, several years later, she celebrates Christmas—at home and her shop—with enviable elegance and élan.

*On the same day she became a shop owner, Tracy Lorton, **above**, purchased this picturesque English-style cottage, **left**. At Christmastime, and always, she fills her house, including the lovely sun-room, **right**, with luscious colors, tempting textures, prized collections, and pleasing seasonal scents.*

ntil three years ago, Tracy Lorton's longtime tradition had been to spend Christmas with her family—parents, brother, and sister—in Aspen. But things changed after she quit her job in New York, moved back to her hometown of Tulsa, and became the proprietor of a fashionable home accessories, tableware, and gift shop.

"When you own a store that does a great share of its business at Christmastime, it is impossible to even *think* of going away for the holidays," Tracy relates.

But rather than lament being tied to Tulsa at Christmas, Tracy decided to put a new twist on that old English proverb—"If the mountain won't come to Mohammed, then Mohammed must go to the mountain." Her twist: Persuade her family to forgo Christmas in the mountains and spend it with her in Tulsa instead.

Last year, to Tracy's delight, her family agreed to do just that. "Once they said yes," she says, "I knew I'd better get busy making the house so irresistible that Aspen would hardly be missed."

And busy she got, not just at home, but at her shop. "I knew that to make everything work, I'd have to do some serious planning," she says. Thus, while spending days, and many nights, preparing her shop for the

*An avid needlepointer, Tracy—in less than two months' time—stitched 25 intricately detailed Santas for the tree, **left**. By next Christmas, she hopes to complete 50 more. The magnificent needlepoint rug in the living room, and another in the dining room, were designed by Tracy but made in Hong Kong. In the dining room, **below**, Tracy and a friend discuss holiday plans.*

annual Christmas rush, she'd simultaneously think of ways to lavish attention on her house.

Whereas many people would blanch at the idea of preparing for Christmas in two places, Tracy was in her element. "Even though it gets hectic," she says, "the holidays are my happiest time of year."

Her house, a deliciously cozy storybook cottage—complete with turret—reflects her yuletide enthusiasms. From the tree in the living room, *left,* to the gift-laden dining table, *above,* the scene is one of glorious abundance.

The aroma of fresh-cut evergreens permeates the house. On the fireplace

Some of my friends were a bit skeptical about my choice of red for the walls, but I decided to take the plunge anyway.

—— TRACY LORTON

Tracy spends much of her free time in her den, **right,** *where pillows made of antique English tapestries, a collection of cow prints, and seasonal decorations add to the room's intimate allure. The handsome black-lacquered* **secretaire, below,** *is home for assorted treasures. Tracy is especially fond of the English antique letter box with its mother-of-pearl inlay.*

mantels in the living room and the den, *right,* Tracy laced the greens with delicate ornaments, long strands of glittering beads, and fetching bows. Intermingled with the aroma of greens are the scents of paper-whites, potted poinsettias, and gorgeous rose topiaries such as the one gracing the antique black-lacquered *secretaire, above.* Tracy uses the elaborately detailed piece to display her treasure trove of tin boxes, leather books, silver pieces, papier-mâché items, and Limoges boxes. A tole lamp, embellished with a crimson tassel, casts a warm glow on the *objets* and holiday accessories.

Collecting is Tracy's grand passion, and she's been at it since she was a little girl. She is particularly enamored of rare and unusual items—the harder to find the better. She travels extensively, in this country and abroad, in search of unique acquisitions for herself and her shop. "Half of the fun of collecting is the search and discovery," she says.

Ranking among her favorite collections are cow prints. A sampling of her beloved bovines, all handsomely framed, furnishes the walls in the den, *right.*

A regard for tradition and fine

It's hard to say whether Tracy's shop, **left** and **below**, is like an extension of her house or vice versa. Both are feasts for the eyes, and both abound with all manner of fine and fascinating things. Of late, to please her many patrons, she has expanded the shop to include a bridal registry and a more extensive line of home furnishings.

Tracy wowed her family by lavishing the dining table, *opposite*, with a lush assortment of silver, crystal, and holiday decorations. Adjuncts to the scene include a chandelier of Gallic origin, an imported French tablecloth, and a fabulous collection of faience.

artisanship led Tracy to develop a fondness for faience, tin-glazed pottery from France. She revels in the distinctive look of each handmade piece and presents her impressive collection of Solanée faience as a focal point in her dining room, *opposite*.

Equally impressive, especially at Christmas, is the dining table itself. The sumptuous centerpiece is composed of a rose and ivy topiary surrounded by glittering ornaments, Limoges boxes, faux jewelery, gem-encrusted napkin rings, antique silverware, heirloom china and crystal, and imported European table linens.

Also adorning the antique table is a mound of small Christmas gifts, each exquisitely wrapped. "I thought it would be pretty, but also fun, because after dinner each member of my family could take a present and open it right there at the table," she says. "It turned out to be a big hit with everyone, and will probably become a new family tradition."

Whether at home or at work, there's no question that Tracy has what it takes to make a big hit. Her store, T.A. Lorton, *above* and *near right*, has been a huge success, almost since the day Tracy became its owner three years ago. Featuring unique lines of European dishware, crystal,

I want my friends and family to come into my house and feel perfectly at home. I love beautiful antiques, but I'm opposed to environments where you have to tiptoe around expensive things.

—— TRACY LORTON

bed and bath linens, lovely christening dresses, antique silver, seldom-met accessories, furniture, and countless other treasures, the store is a mecca for discriminating shoppers.

So successful is T.A. Lorton that Tracy recently expanded the shop to almost double its original size. Her plans now are to offer a complete line of home furnishings, as well as her current selections.

Patrons of the store benefit from the owner's buoyant Christmas spirit and enthusiasm for the holidays. Her gorgeous Christmas window displays have become legendary in Tulsa. Propped with imported tree ornaments, splendid gifts, unequaled seasonal decorations, and plenty of magical sparkle, the windows are irresistible temptations for holiday shoppers passing by.

When asked if she ever tires of her incredibly busy, sometimes frenetic, holiday schedule, Tracy was surprised by the question. "Oh, no," she says. "Half of the fun of Christmas for me is that I get to decorate my house *and* the store." What is the other half? "Actually," she explains, "the most meaningful part of Christmas for me is being with my family."

Happily, for Tracy, she won't have to worry about whether her family will return to Tulsa this Christmas. "We started some new traditions at my house and we're all looking forward to repeating the experience," Tracy reports. □

Index